Meeting the Needs

of

Employees with Disabilities

Resources for Rehabilitation
Winchester, Massachusetts

Resources for Rehabilitation
22 Bonad Road
Winchester, Massachusetts 01890
(781) 368-9094   FAX (781) 368-9096
info@rfr.org   www.rfr.org

Meeting the Needs of Employees with Disabilities, 4th edition

Copyright 2004 by Resources for Rehabilitation, Inc.

ISBN 0-929718-34-8

Resources for Rehabilitation is a nonprofit organization dedicated to providing training and information to professionals and the public about the needs of individuals with disabilities and the resources available to meet those needs.

Library of Congress Cataloging-in-Publication Data

Meeting the Needs of Employees with Disabilities -- 4th ed
  p.   cm.
Includes bibliographical references and index.
ISBN 0-929718-34-8 (alk. paper)
1. Vocational rehabilitation--United States 2. People with disabilities--Employment--United States
3. Self-help devices for people with disabilities--United States--Directories.   I. Resources for Rehabilitation (Organization)
HD7256.U5M445   2004
658.3'0087--dc212   2004002289

For a complete listing of publications available from Resources for Rehabilitation, see pages 205-208.

TABLE OF CONTENTS

HOW TO USE THIS BOOK

The number of people in our society with disabilities and chronic conditions has grown rapidly. At the same time, advances in technology, especially those related to the personal computer, have contributed to the ability of these individuals to continue functioning independently in most aspects of daily life, including work. Although the technology that enables individuals with disabilities to function independently continues to expand, in many instances the individuals themselves, employers, and service providers have not learned about these advances.

This book is designed to provide the information that individuals with disabilities and chronic conditions, employers, and service providers need to ensure that all possible measures have been taken to promote employment. It provides information on a wide variety of organizations, publications, and assistive devices. Individuals have different employment goals and different types and degrees of impairments; therefore, the book is organized so that readers may select the services and devices that are most appropriate to their specific situations.

Each chapter has introductory narrative material, followed by annotated descriptions of organizations and publications, software, and tapes. The chapters that are related to specific impairments also include resources for assistive devices. Descriptions of organizations, publications, software, and tapes, and assistive devices are alphabetical within sections. Although many of the publications described are available in libraries or bookstores, for those who wish to purchase the books by mail, online, or phone, the addresses, phone numbers, and web sites of publishers and distributors are included. Only directories that have timely information and those that are updated regularly are included. Publications that are out of print may be located at libraries or bookstores that specialize in locating out of print books. Unless otherwise noted, all videotapes are produced in VHS format. All of the material is up-to-date and prices were accurate as of the time of publication. However, it is always wise to contact the publisher or manufacturer to obtain the current price, availability, and shipping and handling charges.

The use of "TTY" in the listings indicates a teletypewriter, a special telephone system for individuals who are deaf or have hearing impairments and those who have speech impairments (also known as a "TDD," telecommunication device for the deaf or "TT," text telephone). The use of "V/TTY" indicates that the same telephone number is used for both voice and TTY. Toll-free numbers may begin with "800," "888," "877," or "866." The use of the term alternate formats means that the publication is available in large print, braille, audiocassette, disk, or CD-ROM.

This book does not include information about diseases, health care professionals, psychological aspects of disability, or aspects of everyday living other than employment. For this information, please refer to our other books, including *Resources for People with Disabilities and Chronic Conditions* and *Living with Low Vision: A Resource Guide for People with Sight Loss*, described on pages 205-208 of this volume.

Chapter 1

WORK AND DISABILITY

The value our society places upon work cannot be overstated. The significance society attaches to occupational status in turn has great effects on self-esteem and self-worth. Unfortunately, for most individuals with disabilities, the goal of paid employment has been an elusive one. Although the studies that have assessed the extent of unemployment among people with disabilities vary in their definition of disability itself, all evidence supports the notion that unemployment is all too prevalent for this population group.

The 2000 census revealed that individuals with disabilities are far less likely to be employed than individuals who do not have a disability. The census reported that there were 49.7 million Americans who had a disability. Among those of working age, 16 to 64, close to a fifth reported one or more disabilities in 2000. Among women, 17.6% had a disability; of these only 51.4% were employed compared to 67.3% of their age peers without a disability. Nearly 20% of men reported one or more disabilities; of these only 60.1% were employed compared to 79.9% of their age peers without a disability. People with disabilities were far more likely than people without disabilities to be poor; the respective proportions were 17.6% and 10.6% (Waldrop and Stern: 2003).

An earlier study showed that individuals with disabilities who are employed earn far less than individuals who do not have work disabilities; in 1997, the median earnings for those with disabilities was $17,666 compared to $23,654 for those without a disability. Severity of disability plays a large role in determination of employment status. Those with a severe disability were far less likely than those whose disability is not severe to be employed; the rates are 31.4% and 82.0% respectively (McNeil: 2001).

While it is clear that there are limitations on what employees with disabilities can do, in many instances they are capable of carrying out all of the tasks required for a particular position. Yet social attitudes toward people with disabilities contribute to the high unemployment rate among this group. The stigma attached to disabilities and the fears people have about disabilities must be addressed in order to reach the goal of equal employment opportunities for people with disabilities. Educational programs for members of human resources departments, supervisors, and staff members are an important first step in changing attitudes and overcoming stigma.

HIRING AND RETAINING EMPLOYEES WITH DISABILITIES

Outreach efforts to locate job candidates who have disabilities may take many forms. Positions may be listed with vocational rehabilitation agencies, independent living centers, and other organizations that serve individuals with disabilities. Many of these agencies are listed in the community service section or self help guide in the front of telephone directories. Some direct service organizations work cooperatively with employers to offer job training and placement services. Newsletters and magazines produced by consumer organizations often accept classified advertising. World wide web sites with information for people with disabilities include announcements about available positions. Several organizations offer online resume databases that link employers with prospective employees (see "ORGANIZATIONS" section below). Projects with Industry (see Chapter 2, "Federal Laws and Programs") are federally funded programs that work cooperatively with employers to train and place individuals with disabilities. Community colleges, four year colleges, and universities have offices that serve students with disabilities, refer job candidates to potential employers, and list positions.

When arranging an interview with a person who has a disability, be certain that the entry to the building, the route to the interview site, and the room where the interview takes place are all accessible. Speak to the job candidate just as you would to any other individual. Begin with a handshake and look the candidate in the eyes even if he or she is visually impaired or blind; uses a wheelchair; or is deaf and an interpreter is present. Be certain that questions you ask during an interview are related to the job or job performance. Questions that reflect curiosity about the individual's disability are not appropriate. The Americans with Disabilities Act requires that no questions about the disability be asked until a tentative job offer is made, although questions about the ability to carry out the job are permitted (see Chapter 2, "Federal Laws and Programs"). The candidate may respond that he or she is capable of performing certain tasks with assistive equipment or job modifications.

For individuals who are deaf or hearing impaired, speak normally with your mouth clearly visible, and communicate in writing, if necessary. In some cases, arrangements should be made to have an interpreter present. For individuals who are visually impaired or blind, application forms or tests of skills relevant to the position should be in an accessible format, such as braille or large print, or a reader should be available.

Determining whether an individual can carry out the tasks of a particular position may require that both a job analysis, which describes the specific tasks that the position requires, and a functional assessment, which describes the worker's capabilities and limitations, be performed. The job requirements should then be compared with the candidate's capabilities. If the candidate is capable of carrying out most but not all of the job requirements, it may be possible to restructure the position. For example, an individual who has a speech impairment may be able to carry out all of the tasks of a secretarial position except answering the telephone. The job may be restructured so that the candidate with a speech impairment does more typing than other secretaries, and another secretary takes on the responsibility for answering more telephone calls in exchange for less typing. Some employees have conditions which are progressive; as their conditions change, they may require different accommodations, modifications, or a change in position. In many cases, however, the employee's condition is stable, and no additional modifications will be required unless the job tasks or the physical setting change. Employees with disabilities should be placed in positions with a chance for upward mobility and should be afforded the same opportunities as other employees, including continuing education and training opportunities.

Creativity and flexibility on the part of employers will help employees with disabilities attain their maximum level of productivity. For example, with the widespread use of computers, it is now possible for people who tire easily to work at home on compatible computers and come to the workplace for meetings with colleagues, to turn in their work, and to get new assignments. Such an arrangement enables employees who have difficulty traveling or who tire easily to save their energy for the actual work task. Allowing flexible work schedules also helps employees with disabilities who take public transportation choose the most convenient time to travel.

Personal Assistance Services (PAS) are individuals or devices that enable an individual with a disability to perform tasks that he or she would be able to do if not for the disability. PAS may serve as a reasonable accommodation to help an employee perform a job. Examples of PAS include reading handwritten mail to an individual with a visual impairment; employing sign language interpreters for employees who are deaf; and assigning filing and materials retrieval responsibilities to a co-worker of an individual with a mobility impairment.

No matter what type of work is involved, employees will feel that their concerns are being addressed if they are able to contribute to employer policies regarding affirmative action, modifications, and accommodations for employees with disabilities. A committee composed of employees with and without disabilities can help monitor recruitment efforts and discuss special needs. The committee may wish to produce a guide to help new employees with disabilities or employees who become disabled on the job adjust to the workplace.

People who have recently acquired a disability or chronic condition may go through a series of emotions including depression, anger, and denial. Such responses are normal, but may have a serious impact on the individual's work performance. Ideally, the vocational rehabilitation process will include psychological counseling to help individuals adjust to their condition. Ultimately, most individuals do accept their condition and work to find the appropriate accommodations. In the interim, employees may want to take sick leave or vacation time to adjust to their new status. Self-help groups are one way of helping employees adjust to their disabilities. The practical information and emotional support provided by colleagues may speed the adjustment process and prevent minor problems from growing into major ones. Employers may provide a site for self-help meetings after business hours and allow employees to announce the meetings on company bulletin boards or in newsletters. Newsletters and other company communications should be accessible to employees who are visually impaired or blind.

Cooperation and understanding on the part of co-workers is crucial to creating a setting conducive to maximum productivity. Although much information about a specific employee's disability is of a confidential nature, co-workers should be taught how the disability affects joint work efforts, how to help the employee if an emergency situation such as a fire occurs, and how to be comfortable in normal social interactions.

A good first step toward achieving the goal of a safe, secure workplace is to provide a training program about disabilities for members of the personnel or human resources department, supervisors, and other staff members. The program should describe major types of conditions that cause disability, such as deafness and hearing impairment, mobility impairments, and visual impairment and blindness. An exercise where employees "experience a disability" while they carry out their normal work activities enables them to understand the frustrations, the abilities, and the reactions of others to their impairment. It is possible to simulate hearing loss by using maskers; visual impairment by using glasses that simulate both central and peripheral vision loss; and mobility impairments by using wheelchairs, walkers, and other mobility aids. It is very important that a discussion follow any exercise of this sort to clear up misconceptions; address fears; and describe assistive devices and how they can be used in the specific work setting. A professional from a rehabilitation agency or a private practice, an employee with the impairment, or someone from a center for independent living may provide guidance for the simulation exercise and the discussion. Training programs to heighten disability awareness and overcome negative attitudes go a long way toward improving collegial endeavors in the workplace and increasing productivity.

LOCATING SERVICES

The resources described in this book provide services to organizations and individuals throughout North America. In many instances, large organizations will refer callers to regional, state or provincial, or local affiliates. The state vocational rehabilitation agency, departments of employment training, and information and referral offices of the local United Way are good places to start the process of obtaining services. Some hospitals offer services through their occupational or physical therapy departments, or they may have in-house rehabilitation units. Independent living centers are sources of information, training, and possible job candidates.

Each state has a committee that works to improve employment opportunities for individuals with disabilities and to encourage the cooperation of private businesses in reaching this goal. These committees work with local agencies and committees that have similar goals. Contact the state office that serves people with disabilities or the state vocational rehabilitation agency to learn how to contact the committee in your state. Many municipalities also have commissions that make policy and develop programs for individuals with disabilities.

Many professional societies have established committees to develop policies and assistance for members of their profession who have disabilities. Contact the organizations directly to learn about their services and publications, which may prove useful in making accommodations for current employees and recruiting new employees. In addition, most professional societies now offer services that make sessions at conferences accessible to individuals with disabilities. These services include interpreters for individuals who are deaf or hearing impaired, conference schedules in large print, braille, or on tape, and sighted guides to escort individuals who are visually impaired or blind. Most hotels have rooms that are accessible to people with disabilities. They provide showers that are accessible to wheelchair users and assistive devices such as fire and smoke detectors with visual alerting signals.

Some specialized fields have developed special programs to help employees with disabilities obtain the rehabilitation services and equipment they need. For example, farmers with disabilities may obtain services from "AgrAbility" projects, which are joint ventures between cooperative extension services and private disability organizations. These programs receive federal funding to assist and educate farmers and their families (Willkomm: 1992). "Breaking New Ground," a national resource center for farmers with disabilities, can refer farmers to the nearest "AgrAbility" program (see "ORGANIZATIONS" section below).

Federal employment opportunities for individuals with disabilities are coordinated by the Office of Personnel Management (See "ORGANIZATIONS" section below) through Federal Job Information Centers located in many states, listed in telephone directories under "U.S. Government." Most jobs are obtained competitively through a combination of written examination and evaluation of education and experience. When necessary, the government provides readers or makes examinations available in braille, large print, or on audiocassette. Some individuals are given an opportunity to demonstrate their abilities through special appointing techniques called "700-hour trial appointment" or "excepted appointment." Once the individual has successfully completed a trial or served two years in an excepted appointment, his or her job may be noncompetitively converted to a competitive appointment.

The U.S. Department of Veterans Affairs, U.S. Department of Labor, and veterans services organizations promote the vocational rehabilitation and employment of veterans with disabilities through national, state, and local efforts. Federal laws such as the Vietnam Veterans' Readjustment Assistance Act and Title I of the Americans with Disabilities Act support the employment of veterans with disabilities (see Chapter 2, "Federal Laws and Programs"). The Veterans' Readjustment Appointment (VRA) is a special authority by which veterans may be appointed to federal jobs without competition; however, basic employment qualifications must be met. The VRA applies to Vietnam and post-Vietnam era veterans and any veteran who has a service-connected disability of 30%. Time limits may apply. The Small Business Administration (SBA) is conducting a study to determine how the SBA can increase opportunities for disabled veterans. Many states also offer services through their State Veterans Employment Service (found in telephone directories under state government listings).

REHABILITATION

The rehabilitation process helps individuals who have functional impairments or chronic conditions to continue working and living independently. Rehabilitation services may include counseling, job placement, provision of assistive technology, vocational training to remain in a current position or to learn a new skill (including postsecondary education), modifying the work environment, and transportation services. Many individuals who were previously thought to be too disabled to receive services are now successfully rehabilitated (de Jong and Batavia: 1990).

Rehabilitation services are provided by both public and private agencies. In the United States, each state is required by law to have a public agency that is responsible for providing vocational rehabilitation services. In about half of the states, there are separate agencies to serve people who are visually impaired or blind. In the remaining states, services for people who are visually impaired or blind are provided within the general vocational rehabilitation agency. The federal government provides financial support for rehabilitation services and sets standards for service delivery, as required by the Rehabilitation Act of 1973 and its amendments (see Chapter 2, "Federal Laws and Programs") and administered by the Rehabilitation Services Administration. The federal government requires that individuals sign an Individualized Written Rehabilitation Plan that indicates they approve of the rehabilitation strategy developed jointly with counselors in state rehabilitation agencies. Many rehabilitation professionals provide services independently on a fee-for-service basis. In some instances, state rehabilitation agencies develop the rehabilitation program and then contract with professionals in private practices or agencies to provide services to the client.

The types of professionals that provide services to people with disabilities include vocational rehabilitation counselors, rehabilitation engineers, physiatrists, occupational therapists, and physical therapists. These professionals work in public or private rehabilitation agencies, in private practice, in hospitals, and in rehabilitation programs operated by businesses or unions.

Vocational rehabilitation counselors evaluate individuals who have been referred to determine eligibility for services. Eligible individuals and the vocational rehabilitation counselors jointly develop a rehabilitation program that will enable the clients to continue functioning and working. Many individuals with disabilities need retraining to return to their previous position or to obtain a different type of position. Vocational rehabilitation counselors help make the contacts and placements necessary to attain these goals and arrange for enrollment in training programs. In addition, they help obtain necessary medical services and equipment. When the client obtains a position, the counselor may conduct an analysis of the position, the work site, and the individual's needs in order to determine what modifications or assistive devices, if any, are needed. They follow up after placement to be certain that the situation is satisfactory to both employee and employer. Some private companies employ vocational rehabilitation counselors as part of their own in-house staff.

Rehabilitation engineers specialize in the design of devices that enable people with disabilities to function at their maximum level of independence. They develop robotic devices and other computer driven devices that serve as substitutes for the function that was lost as a result of injury or disease. They may consult on individual cases to adapt wheelchairs or other devices to the specific needs of the client.

Physiatrists are physicians who specialize in rehabilitation medicine and design individual treatment plans for people with physical conditions that cause disabilities. *Physical therapists* evaluate the individual's physical condition and the dysfunction it causes and prescribe treatments such as traction, manipulation, heat or cold therapy, exercise, or massage. *Occupational therapists* teach individuals with disabilities how to conduct the activities of daily living, including those necessary for the workplace.

Employers can work effectively with rehabilitation agencies by keeping in close contact with the placement office, listing available positions, and inquiring about new candidates. Employers may also make referrals for services for current employees who have recently acquired disabilities. Working in conjunction with the vocational rehabilitation counselor who carries out functional assessments of the employee, the employer will obtain the information needed to decide whether the employee can continue to carry out his or her former job with or without modifications; learn about accommodations and assistive technology; and consider the possibility of job restructuring or transfer to a different position.

Occupational physicians and nurses are well advised to learn about the availability of local rehabilitation agencies and service providers. Knowing how and when to refer employees with injuries and disabilities for rehabilitation can help return employees to the workplace and result in financial savings for the employer. Returning a worker to the position that he or she held previously, even with job modifications, is usually less costly than training a new employee and paying disability benefits to the injured worker. Prompt referral for rehabilitation is crucial, as most studies indicate that the longer the lapse between injury and rehabilitation, the less likely it is that the employee will return to work. Prompt referrals for rehabilitation indicate that the employer intends to retain the employee, thereby enhancing his or her motivation and self-esteem.

CONCLUSION

Legal mandates to remove barriers to employment for people with disabilities, changes in social attitudes, and rapid advances in technology all suggest that employment opportunities for people with disabilities will improve in the future. It is important that employers, co-workers, rehabilitation professionals, physicians, and the individuals with disabilities themselves learn about the many options available that can result in appropriate employment opportunities. Using the many services and products described in this book will help to ensure that individuals with disabilities receive the employment opportunities that they are entitled to and that society benefits from their talents.

References

de Jong, Gerben and Andrew Batavia
1990   "The Americans with Disabilities Act and the Current State of U.S. Disability Policy"
        Journal of Disability Policy Studies 1(Fall):3:65-74
McNeil, John M.
2001   Americans With Disabilities 1997 Washington, DC: U.S. Bureau of the Census
        Current Population Reports P70-73
Waldrop, Judith and Sharon M. Stern
2003   Disability Status 2000 U.S. Census Bureau March
Willkomm, Therese
1992   "Farming with a Disability" Technology and Disability 1(4):54-62

ORGANIZATIONS

American Counseling Association (ACA)
5999 Stevenson Avenue
Alexandria, VA 22304
(800) 347-6647   (703) 823-6862 (TTY)
FAX (800) 473-2329   www.counseling.org

A professional membership organization with special divisions for rehabilitation, employment counseling, and career development. Membership, $125.00, includes subscriptions to monthly journal, "Counseling Today," and "Journal of Counseling and Development," published quarterly. The American Rehabilitation Counseling Association (ARCA) is a division of the ACA that promotes excellence in rehabilitation counseling of individuals with disabilities. Membership, $70.00, includes newsletter, "Rehabilitation Quarterly" and quarterly journal, "Rehabilitation Counseling Bulletin."

American Indian Rehabilitation Research and Training Center (AIRRTC)
Institute for Human Development
Northern Arizona University
PO Box 5630
Flagstaff, AZ 86011-5630
(928) 523-4791   (928) 523-1695 (TTY)   FAX (928) 523-9127
priscilla.sanderson@nau.edu   www.nau.edu/ihd/airrtc

Conducts research and training to improve vocational rehabilitation services for American Indians with disabilities. Publishes resource and training manuals, directories, and research reports.

American Self-Help Clearinghouse
100 Hanover Avenue, Suite 202
Cedar Knolls, NJ 07927
(973) 326-6789   FAX (973) 326-9467   www.selfhelpgroups.org

Provides information and contacts for national self-help groups, information on model groups, individuals who are starting new networks, and state or local self-help clearinghouses.

Ask Able
askable@askvrd.org

This web site enables users to ask questions on a variety of topics related to disabilities. An appropriate expert will provide an answer. Free

Breaking New Ground Resource Center and Outreach Center
Purdue University
1146 ABE Building
West Lafayette, IN 47907-1146
(800) 825-4264   (765) 494-5088 (V/TTY)   FAX (765) 496-1356
www.breakingnewground.info

A federally funded research center that investigates ways to improve opportunities for employment of farmers with disabilities. Provides assistive technology and outreach. Newsletter, "Breaking New Ground," available in standard print and on audiocassette. Free

Center for an Accessible Society
Exploding Myths, Inc.
2980 Beech Street
San Diego, CA 92107
(619) 232-2727   (619) 234-3130 (TTY)   FAX (619) 234-3135
infor@accessiblesociety.org   www.accessiblesociety.org

This federally funded project disseminates information to the public on topics related to new developments in accessibility and independent living. Distributes a free "E-Letter."

Cornell University Program on Employment and Disability
New York State School of Industrial and Labor Relations, Extension Division
106 ILR Extension Building
Ithaca, NY 14853
(607) 255-7797   (607) 255-2891 (TTY)   FAX (607) 255-2763
ilru_ped@cornell.edu   www.ilr.cornell.edu/ped

This program seeks to improve employment practices covered by Title I of the Americans with Disabilities Act. Produces and disseminates publications on Title I, transition from school to work, and supported employment. Catalogue available on the web site. Conducts research, provides technical assistance, and conducts training programs for employers throughout the U.S. and abroad.

EARN The Employer Assistance Referral Network
c/o CESSI
6858 Old Dominion Drive, Suite 250
McLean, VA 22101
(866) 327-6669 (V/TTY)   FAX (703) 448-7545   earn@earnworks.com
www.earnworks.com

Sponsored by the U.S, Department of Labor, this program links employers who have positions available with individuals who place people with disabilities in jobs.

Entry Point!
Technology and Disability
American Association for the Advancement of Science (AAAS)
1200 New York Avenue, NW
Washington, DC 20005
(202) 326-6649 (V/TTY)   FAX (202) 371-9849   lsummers@aaas.org
www.entrypoint.org

This program provides summer and school year internships for undergraduate and graduate students with disabilities majoring in science, engineering, computer science, or mathematics. Placements with businesses and government agencies throughout the country.

Foundation for Science and Disability (FSD)
c/o Dr. E.C. Keller, Jr.
Biology Department
West Virginia University
Morgantown, WV 26506-6057
(304) 293-5201, ext. 2513   ekeller@wvu.edu
www.as.wvu.edu/~scidis/organizations/FSD_brochure.html

An organization that seeks to promote employment opportunities for scientists, students, and other professionals with disabilities. Provides technical assistance to employers, educational institutions, government agencies, and other scientific bodies. Sponsors an award program for undergraduate and graduate students majoring in science, math, or engineering. Membership, $25.00; students, $5.00. "FSD Newsletter" published three times a year.

Institute for Community Inclusion (ICI)
University of Massachusetts Boston
100 Morrissey Boulevard
Boston, MA 02125
(617) 287-4300   (617) 287-4350 (TTY)   FAX (617) 287-4352
ici@umb.edu   www.communityinclusion.org

Funded by the U.S. Department of Labor, this center works to improve opportunities for people with disabilities to obtain employment in the community. Sends biweekly "E-Announcements." Resources for employers available on web site.

International Association of Rehabilitation Professionals (IARP)
3540 Soquel Avenue, Suite A
Santa Cruz, CA 95062
(800) 240-9059   (831) 464-4892
FAX (831) 576-1417   shiela@btfenterprises.com   www.rehabpro.org

A membership organization for rehabilitation professionals who work as case managers, in long term disability, and consulting on disability management, life care planning, and Americans with Disabilities Act compliance. Holds annual meeting. Membership, $107.00, plus local chapter fee; includes journal "RehabPro." A member directory is available on the web site.

National Business and Disability Council
201 IU Willets Road
Albertson, NY 11507
(516) 465-1515   FAX (516) 465-3730
nbdc@resume-link.com   www.business-disability.com

This organization aims to integrate people with disabilities into the corporate world. Individuals with disabilities, who hold at least a two-year college degree, may register and post their resumes on this free database, accessible to employers who are members of the National Business and Disability Council. Individuals may register by mail or on the web site. Employers post job openings on the site. The council also provides training, consultation, and technical assistance. Informational hotline, (516) 465-1519.

National Easter Seals Society
230 West Monroe Street, Suite 1800
Chicago, IL 60606-4802
(800) 221-6827   (312) 726-6200   (312) 726-4258 (TTY)
FAX (312) 726-1494   info@easter-seals.org
www.easter-seals.org

Promotes research, education, and rehabilitation for people with physical disabilities and speech and language problems.

National Institute on Disability and Rehabilitation Research (NIDRR)
U.S. Department of Education
400 Maryland Avenue, SW
Washington, DC 20202
(202) 205-8134   (202) 205-8198 (TTY)   FAX (202) 205-8515
www.ed.gov/about/offices/list/osers/nidrr/about.html

A federal agency that supports research into various aspects of disability and rehabilitation, including demographic analyses, social science research, and the development of assistive devices. Grant programs are announced in the "Federal Register" (see "PUBLICATIONS" section below) or may be obtained directly from NIDRR. Funds regional Disability and Business Technical Assistance Centers (DBTAC) that provide publications, assistance, and training (800) 949-4232 (V/TTY); www.adata.org

National Organization on Disability (NOD)
910 16th Street, NW, Suite 600
Washington, DC 20006
(202) 293-5960   (202) 293-5968 (TTY)
FAX (202) 293-7999   ability@nod.org   www.nod.org

An organization dedicated to achieving the full participation of people with disabilities in all aspects of community life. Works with a network of local agencies to achieve this goal. Provides technical assistance and maintains an informational database. Sends a bimonthly electronic newsletter, "E-Newsletter." Free

National Rehabilitation Association (NRA)
633 South Washington Street
Alexandria, VA 22314
(703) 836-0850   (703) 836-0849 (TTY)
FAX (703) 836-0848   info@nationalrehab.org   www.nationalrehab.org

A membership organization for rehabilitation professionals and independent living center affiliates. Includes special divisions for independent living, counseling, job placement, etc. Legislative Network Alerts appear on NRA's web site. Membership, professionals, $110.0; organizations, $500.00; includes "Journal of Rehabilitation" and bimonthly newsletter, "Contemporary Rehab."

National Rehabilitation Information Center (NARIC)
4200 Forbes Boulevard, Suite 202
Lanham, MD 20706
(800) 346-2742   (301) 459-5900   (301) 459-5984 (TTY)
naricinfo@heitechservices.com   www.naric.com

A federally funded center that responds to telephone and mail inquiries about disabilities and support services. Maintains REHABDATA, a database with publications and research references; searches may be done online. Online descriptions of research projects supported by NIDRR (see above). "Rehabdata-Connections" is a monthly bibliography sent by e-mail. Free. Some NARIC publications are available on the web site.

National Science Foundation (NSF)
Directorate for Computer and Information Science and Engineering (CISE)
4201 Wilson Boulevard, Suite 11105
Arlington, VA 22230
(703) 292-8930   FAX (703) 292-9073   cisewebteam@nsf.gov
www.nsf.gov

Supports "Facilitation Awards for Scientists and Engineers with Disabilities," which provide funding for special equipment for scientists and students to work on projects funded by NSF.

Office of Disability Employment Policy (ODEP)
U.S. Department of Labor
Employment Standards Administration
U.S. Department of Labor
200 Constitution Avenue, NW
Washington, DC 20210
(866) 487-2365   (877) 889-5627 (TTY)
(202) 693-7880   (202) 693-7881 (TTY)   FAX (202) 693-7888
www.dol.gov/odep

This federal agency works to increase opportunities for youths and adults with disabilities to obtain employment. ODEP works to expand opportunities thorough education, training, employment support, and technical assistance for individuals. ODEP also builds partnerships with businesses and government agencies to increase awareness of the benefits of hiring people with disabilities. Sponsors the Small Business Self-Employment (SBSES) program that provides information to people with disabilities who wish to work for themselves [(800) 525-7234 or (800) 232-9675 (V/TTY)]. The Workforce Recruitment Program enables employers to obtain resumes of college student with disabilities from across the country. Interested employers may contact kravitz.betsy@dol.gov for more information. College students should contact their career counseling or disability services office at their college.

Office of Personnel Management (OPM)
Federal Job Information Center
1900 E Street, NW, Room 1416
Washington, DC 20415
(202) 606-1221   (202) 606-2532 (TTY)   FAX (202) 606-5049)
www.opm.gov/disability

Assists individuals with disabilities in finding positions in the federal civil service. Call to request information and application forms. Federal Job Information Centers are located throughout the country. Look in the telephone directory under "U.S. Government Listings." Information about open examinations and vacancy announcements is available at www.usajobs.opm.gov

Office of Workers' Compensation Program (OWCP)
Employment Standards Administration
U.S. Department of Labor
200 Constitution Avenue, NW
Washington, DC 20210
(202) 693-0031   FAX (202) 693-1497
www.dol.gov/esa/owcp_org

Provides vocational rehabilitation services and workers' compensation benefits to federal workers who are disabled as a result of job related injury or illness. A rehabilitation counselor and the client jointly establish a rehabilitation program which may include medical rehabilitation, vocational counseling, training, or job modification. OWCP works with employers to develop return-to-work programs. Regional OWCP offices throughout the country. Administers the Federal Employees Compensation Act (FECA) for employees of the federal government who are injured on the job.

Projects with Industry (PWI)
Office of Special Education and Rehabilitation Services (OSERS)
U.S. Department of Education
400 Maryland Avenue, SW, Room 3332
Washington, DC 20202-2740
(202) 205-8922   FAX (202) 260-9424   lavanna.weems@ed.gov
www.ed.gov/programs/rsapwi/index.html

A federally funded program authorized under the Rehabilitation Act, PWI funds programs that expand job opportunities for individuals with disabilities. Services include training, support, job development, and job placement.

Rehabilitation Research and Training Center on Demographics and Statistics
Ives Hall, Room 331
Cornell University
Ithaca, NY 14853
(607) 255-5702   (607) 255-2891 (TTY)   FAX (607) 255-3274
ajh29@cornell.edu   www.disabilitystatistics.org

This federally funded center explores the reliability of databases related to disability and studies the potential to improve these data and future databases.

Rehabilitation Research and Training Center on Workplace Supports
Virginia Commonwealth University
PO Box 842011
Richmond, VA 23284-2011
(804) 828-1851   (804) 828-2494 (TTY)   FAX (804) 828-2193
tcblanke@mail.vcu.edu   www.worksupport.com

This federally funded center conducts research on workplace supports and supplies many articles on the topic on its web site. Also sends an electronic newsletter with information updates. Free. The web site features information on accommodations, disability management, bridges to employment, supported employment, workforce diversity, and workforce training.

Rehabilitation Services Administration (RSA)
U.S. Department of Education
400 Maryland Avenue, SW, Room 3329-MES
Washington, DC 20202-2251
(202) 205-5482   FAX (202) 205-9874
www.ed.gov/about/offices/list/osers/osers/about.html

The principal federal agency mandated to carry out the provisions of the Rehabilitation Act of 1973 and its amendments.

Small Business Administration (SBA)
6302 Fairview Road, Suite 300
Charlotte, NC 28210
(800) 827-5722   (704) 344-6640 (TTY)   FAX (202) 205-7064
answerdesk@sba.gov   www.sba.gov

The SBA provides limited direct loans to businesses owned by individuals with disabilities that meet certain guidelines. The local SBA office is listed in the "U.S. Government" section of the telephone directory. Provides online guidelines for small businesses to comply with the Americans with Disabilities Act. Web site also provides shareware and freeware software for people with disabilities. Applicants for services from the SBA may apply online and mail to their regional SBA office.

T-TAP Training and Technical Assistance for Providers
Virginia Commonwealth University
1314 West Main Street
Richmond, VA 23284
(804) 828-1851   (804) 828-2494 (TTY)   FAX (804) 828-2193
kinge@atlas.vcu.edu   www.t-tap.org

Funded by the Office of Disability Employment Policy of the U.S. Department of Labor, this project aims to assist community rehabilitation programs that place clients with disabilities in segregated settings to job placements in integrated settings through the use of customized employment strategies and to increase the wages of individuals who currently earn less than minimum wages.

United Cerebral Palsy Association (UCPA)
1660 L Street, NW, Suite 700
Washington, DC 20036
(800) 872-5827   (202) 776-0406   (202) 973-7197
FAX (202) 776-0414   webmaster@ucpa.org   www.ucpa.org

Member groups throughout the country provide treatment, information, education, and counseling. UCPA helps job seekers find a job by assisting with preparing a resume, providing career information, and providing job opportunities

Vocational Rehabilitation Services
Veterans Benefits Administration
Department of Veterans Affairs (VA)
810 Vermont Avenue, NW
Washington, DC 20420
(202) 273-5400   (800) 827-1000 (connects with regional office)
FAX (202) 273-7485   www.va.gov

Provides education and rehabilitation assistance and independent living services to veterans with service related disabilities through offices located in every state as well as regional centers, medical centers, and insurance centers. VONAPP (VA Online Application) enables veterans to apply for benefits on the Internet.

World Institute on Disability (WID)
510 16th Street, Suite 100
Oakland, CA 94612-1502
(510) 763-4100   (510) 208-9496 (TTY)   FAX (510) 763-4109
webpoohbah@wid.org   www.wid.org

A public policy center founded and operated by individuals with disabilities, WID conducts research, public education, and training. It also develops model programs related to disability. It deals with issues such as personal assistance, public transportation, employment, and access to health care. WID's Research and Training Center on Independent Living and Disability Policy is a federally funded center that studies federal independent living initiatives and community integration issues. Publishes a semi-annual newsletter, "Equity," which focuses on economic development and the disability community; "Open Line," a quarterly newsletter which reports on policy developments in access to telecommunications for people with disabilities; and "Impact," a semi-annual newsletter.

Barn Builders
Breaking New Ground Resource Center
Purdue University
1146 Agricultural Engineering Building
West Lafayette, IN 47907-1146
(800) 825-4264   (765) 494-5088 (V/TTY)   FAX (765) 496-1356
www.breakingnewground.info

This directory of farmers and ranchers with disabilities and caregivers connects individuals with others who are willing to share their experiences. $10.00

Career Advancement Strategies and Tools
Program Development Associates
PO Box 2038
Syracuse, NY 13220-2038
(800) 543-2119   FAX (315) 452-0710   www.pdassoc.com

This book guides service providers and individuals with disabilities through career planning, assessing job satisfaction, developing a support network, and obtaining experience and training. Includes worksheets that help to individualize the plan. $49.00

Careers & the DisABLED
Equal Opportunity Publications
445 Broad Hollow Road, Suite 425
Melville, NY 11747
(631) 421-9421   FAX (631) 421-0359   info@eop.com
www.eop.com

This quarterly magazine features career guidance articles, role model profiles, and lists of companies looking for qualified job candidates. Offers Online Resume Database which matches readers with advertisers who are recruiting employees. One year, $12.00; two years, $22.00.

Directory of Grants for Organizations Serving People with Disabilities
Research Grant Guides
12798 West Forest Hill Boulevard, Suite 304
West Palm Beach, FL 33414
(561) 795-6129   FAX (561) 795-7794
www.researchgrant.com

This directory provides information about funding available from foundations, corporations, and government agencies. $69.00

Disabilities in the Workplace: Working Out
Films for the Humanities and Sciences
PO Box 2053
Princeton, NJ 08543-2053
(800) 257-5126   FAX (609) 671-0266
custserv@films.com   www.films.com

This film depicts four individuals with different disabilities as they cope with employment setting. Enables colleagues who do not have disabilities to gain a better understanding of what it is like to work with a disability. 24 minutes. Videotape, $89.95; DVD, $114.95.

Disability Employment 101
Office of Special Education and Rehabilitation Services (OSERS)
U.S. Department of Education
400 Maryland Avenue, SW
Washington, DC 20202
www.ed.gov/about/offices/list/osers/products/employmentguide/index.htm

Written jointly with the U.S. Chamber of Commerce, this publication provides information for business leaders about programs and resources to help them hire people with disabilities. Free. Also available on the web site.

Doing It Their Way: Employer Perspectives on Workplace Support
HEATH Resource Center
George Washington University
2121 K Street, NW, Suite 220
Washington, DC 20037
(800) 544-3284 (V/TTY)   (202) 973-0904 (V/TTY)
FAX (202) 973-0908   askheath@heath.gwu.edu   www.heath.gwu.edu

This paper discusses the relationship between organizational development, human resources, and organizational supports for employees with disabilities as well as the employer's perspectives on these issues. Free. Also available on the web site.

Encyclopedia of Disability and Rehabilitation
by Arthur E. Dell Orto and Robert P. Marinelli (eds.)
Gale Group
PO Box 9187
Farmington Hills, MI 48333-9187
(800) 877-4253   FAX (800) 414-5043
galeord@galegroup.com   www.gale.com

Written by a variety of experts in the field of disability, this reference book includes articles ranging from AIDS to stroke, advocacy to wheelchairs, and aging to work. $140.00

Enterprising Ideas
Breaking New Ground Resource Center
Purdue University
1146 Agricultural Engineering Building
West Lafayette, IN 47907-1146
(800) 825-4264   (765) 494-5088 (V/TTY)   FAX (765) 496-1356
www.breakingnewground.info

This book profiles farmers and ranchers with disabilities who have chosen alternative careers, such as running commercial greenhouses or farm vacations. $10.00

Entrepreneurship, Self-Employment and Disabilities
Program Development Associates
PO Box 2038
Syracuse, NY 13220-2038
(800) 543-2119   FAX (315) 452-0710   www.pdassoc.com

This videotape demonstrates how individuals with disabilities use their motivations and skills as well as support from others to start small businesses. 33 minutes $59.00

Federal Register
New Orders, Superintendent of Documents
PO Box 371954
Pittsburgh, PA 15250-7954
(866) 512-1800   FAX (202) 512-2250   gpoaccess@gpo.gov
bookstore.gpo.gov

A federal publication printed every weekday with notices of all regulations and legal notices issued by federal agencies. Domestic subscriptions, $764.00 annually. Also available on the web site at no charge.

Foundations of the Vocational Rehabilitation Process
by Stanford E. Rubin and Richard T. Roessler
Pro-Ed
8700 Shoal Creek Boulevard
Austin, TX 78758
(800) 897-3202   (512) 451-3246   FAX (800) 397-7633
www.proedinc.com

A textbook with complete coverage of the development of vocational rehabilitation programs in the U.S., legislative history, and procedures used by professionals to conduct client assessments and deliver services. $39.00

Functional Capacities Checklist
Elliott and Fitzpatrick
1135 Cedar Shoals Drive
Athens, GA 30605
(800) 843-4977   FAX (706) 227-2204
orders@elliottfitzpatrick.com   www.elliottfitzpatrick.com

Worksheetts designed to determine how clients view their own physical capacities.   Package of 50, $15.00.

Given the Opportunity
Films for the Humanities and Sciences
PO Box 2053
Princeton, NJ 08543-2053
(800) 257-5126   FAX (609) 671-0266
custserv@films.com   www.films.com

A videotape that focuses on interactions between employees with disabilities and those without disabilities. Representative of major companies and employees with disabilities each present their own perspectives. 24 minutes. $99.95

Helping Hands
Fanlight Productions
Meridian Education Corporation
PO Box 911
Monmouth Junction, NJ 08852-0911
(800) 727-5507   FAX (888) 340-5507
fanlight@fanlight.com   www.fanlight.com

This videotape demonstrates that simple workplace modifications can accommodate the needs of workers with disabilities. 37 minutes. Purchase, $149.00; rental for one day $60.00; for one week $100.00.

Job Interviewing for People with Disabilities
Fanlight Productions
Meridian Education Corporation
PO Box 911
Monmouth Junction, NJ 08852-0911
(800) 727-5507   FAX (888) 340-5507
fanlight@fanlight.com   www.fanlight.com

This videotape demonstrates how people with disabilities should focus on their skills during job interviews and not on their disabilities. It discusses attitude toward the job, rights according to the law, and tips for staying positive. 30 minutes. $89.95

Job Search Handbook for People with Disabilities
Jist Publishing
8902 Otis Avenue
Indianapolis, IN 46216
(800) 648-5478   (317) 613-4200
FAX (317) 613-4309   info@jist.com   www.jist.com

This book provides guidance on finding the right career, skills assessment, job searching techniques, and obtaining accommodations on the job. $16.95

Job Training and Placement Report
Impact Publications, Inc.
PO Box 322
Waupaca, WI 54981
(715) 258-2448   FAX (715) 258-9048
info@impact-publications.com   www.impact-publications.com

A monthly newsletter with information about funding sources for job training and placement services plus practical information about how to solve problems commonly encountered by rehabilitation professionals. One year, $149.00; 2 years, $269.00.

Journal of Rehabilitation Research and Development (JRRD)
Scientific and Technical Publications Section
Rehabilitation Research and Development Service
103 South Gay Street, 5th Floor
Baltimore, MD 21202
(410) 962-1800   FAX (410) 962-9670   pubs@vard.org
www.vard.org

A bimonthly journal that includes articles on disability, rehabilitation, sensory aids, gerontology, and disabling conditions. Available in standard print and on the web site. Free

Key Changes
Fanlight Productions
Meridian Education Corporation
PO Box 911
Monmouth Junction, NJ 08852-0911
(800) 727-5507   FAX (888) 340-5507
fanlight@fanlight.com   www.fanlight.com

This videotape portrays Lisa Thorson, a vocalist who experienced a spinal cord injury and continues performing in her chosen profession. 28 minutes. $149.00

Making Career Decisions Following a Disability
Breaking New Ground Resource Center
Purdue University
1146 Agricultural Engineering Building
West Lafayette, IN 47907-1146
(800) 825-4264   (765) 494-5088 (V/TTY)   FAX (765) 496-1356
www.breakingnewground.info

This book provides practical suggestions to help farmers and ranchers make career decisions. Contains worksheets, sample cover letters, resumes, etc. $30.00

Making Self-Employment Work for People with Disabilities
by Cary Griffin and David Hammis
Brookes Publishing Company
PO Box 10624
Baltimore, MD 21285-9945
(800) 638-3775   FAX (410) 337-8539
custserv@pbrookes.com   www.brookespublishing.com

This book is a guide through the process of establishing a small business. It discusses business planning, marketing strategies, financial aspects, and the development of support systems. $35.00

More Than a Job: Securing Satisfying Careers for People with Disabilities
by Paul Wehman and John Kregel (eds.)
Brookes Publishing Company
PO Box 10624
Baltimore, MD 21285-0624
(800) 638-3775   FAX (410) 337-8539
custserv@pbrookes.com   www.brookespublishing.com

This book presents a consumer perspective on disability and employment. Covers employment strategies such as supported employment, vocational training, and assistive technology. $34.95

National AgrAbility Project
Breaking New Ground Resource Center
Purdue University
1146 Agricultural Engineering Building
West Lafayette, IN 47907-1146
(800) 825-4264   (765) 494-5088 (V/TTY)   FAX (765) 496-1356
www.breakingnewground.info

This videotape provides an overview of this project and the services and programs available to agricultural workers with disabilities. 15 minutes. Open captioned version available. $20.00

Resources for People with Disabilities and Chronic Conditions
Resources for Rehabilitation
22 Bonad Road
Winchester, Massachusetts 01890
(781) 368-9094   FAX (781) 368-9096   info@rfr.org
www.rfr.org

A comprehensive resource guide with information on how to find services, laws affecting individuals with disabilities, and making everyday living easier. Chapters on hearing and speech impairments, spinal cord injuries, low back pain, diabetes, multiple sclerosis, vision impairment and blindness, and epilepsy include information about the disease or condition; psychological aspects of the condition; professional service providers; environmental adaptations; assistive devices; and descriptions of organizations, publications, and products. $56.95 (See order form on last page of this book.)

Resumes and Applications for People with Disabilities
Films for the Humanities and Sciences
PO Box 2053
Princeton, NJ 08543-2053
(800) 257-5126   FAX (609) 671-0266
custserv@films.com   www.films.com

This videotape covers how to use your resume or application effectively to emphasize your skills and when and how to discuss your disabilities. Also discusses protections provided by the Americans with Disabilities Act. 30 minutes. $89.95

Six Steps to Employment
Program Development Associates
PO Box 2038
Syracuse, NY 13220-2038
(800) 543-2119   FAX (315) 452-0710   www.pdassoc.com

This book discusses how people with disabilities can overcome obstacles and show their effectiveness to potential employers. Includes sample resumes and letters. $29.95

Supervising an Employee with a Disability
Program Development Associates
PO Box 2038
Syracuse, NY 13220-2038
(800) 543-2119   FAX (315) 452-0710   www.pdassoc.com

This videotape provides practical information through the real-life experiences of supervisors and their employees. 20 minutes. Includes instructor's guide, handouts, and a videotape of training exercises. $195.00

Us and Them
Fanlight Productions
Medial Library
PO Box 1084
Harriman, NY 10926
(800) 343-5540   FAX (845) 774-2945   orders@fanlight.com
www.fanlight.com

This videotape about relationships between people who have disabilities and those who do not. 32 minutes, black and white. Purchase, $69.00; rental for one day $50.00.

A Videoguide to (Dis)Ability Awareness
Fanlight Productions
Medial Library
PO Box 1084
Harriman, NY 10926
(800) 343-5540   FAX (845) 774-2945   orders@fanlight.com
www.fanlight.com

This videotape promotes awareness of the abilities of individuals with disabilities and how to identify and remove unintentional barriers in an organization. Includes tips for interacting with individuals who are blind or have hearing loss. Open or closed captioned. 25 minutes. $199.00

Chapter 2

FEDERAL LAWS AND PROGRAMS

On July 26, 1990, the *Americans with Disabilities Act* (ADA) was passed. Considered the most important piece of civil rights legislation in recent years, the ADA (P.L. 101-336) increases the steps employers must take to accommodate employees with disabilities. According to the law, an individual with a disability is a person who has a physical or mental impairment that substantially limits one or more major activities; someone who has had such an impairment; or someone who is regarded as having such an impairment. Individuals with chronic conditions, such as cancer, epilepsy, and AIDS, or disfigurements are also protected by the law. Although the definition of disability is very broad, it is based upon previous legislation (such as the Rehabilitation Act) and a large body of case law.

Title I of the ADA prohibits discrimination against individuals with disabilities who are otherwise qualified to carry out the essential functions of a position, with or without reasonable accommodations. The employer determines what is considered to be the essential functions of the position by writing a job description prior to advertising the position. "Reasonable accommodations" include making existing facilities accessible or job restructuring, which means reassignment to a different position; modification or provision of equipment; training; or provision of interpreters and readers. The provisions of this section apply to employers with 15 or more employees.

Discrimination is defined as limiting the opportunities of a job applicant or employee; engaging in an arrangement with a referral agency, union, or other organization that discriminates against individuals with disabilities; not making reasonable accommodations for an applicant or employee; using tests or other screening criteria that eliminate individuals with disabilities, unless the criteria are job related; failing to administer tests to individuals with disabilities in the most effective manner to accommodate the disability, unless the disability would prevent the person from carrying out the essential functions of the job. Inquiries about a disability and pre-employment medical examinations are prohibited prior to the conditional offer of employment; questions related to the ability to carry out job functions are allowed. Medical examinations may be conducted following a conditional offer of employment only if all employees, including those without disabilities, are required to undergo such examinations. Information collected about disabilities must be kept confidential except to inform supervisors about necessary work restrictions and accommodations regarding safety and first aid.

Employers are protected from "undue hardship" in complying with the ADA. The financial situation of the employer and the size and type of business are considered when determining whether an accommodation would constitute "undue hardship." A 1995 Harris poll (cited in Kaye: 1998) found that 81% of employer had made accommodations for workers with disabilities compared to 51% in 1986).

Title II of the ADA prohibits discrimination by public entities (i.e., local and state governments) and requires that individuals with disabilities be entitled to the same rights and benefits of public programs as other individuals regardless of the number of employees such entities employ. Title II is enforced by the Civil Right Division of the U.S. Department of

Justice. Complainants need not exhaust administrative procedures if problems remain unresolved and may elect to proceed with a private suit at any time.

Title III requires that public accommodations, businesses, and services be accessible to individuals with disabilities. Public accommodations are broadly defined to include places such as hotels and motels, theatres, museums, schools, shopping centers and stores, banks, restaurants, and professional service providers' offices. Effective January 26, 1993, most new construction for public accommodations must be accessible to individuals with disabilities.

Title IV of the ADA requires that telephone companies provide relay services 24 hours a day, seven days a week for individuals with hearing or speech impairments. Relay services enable individuals who have text telephones (also called teletypewriters or telecommunication devices for the deaf) or another computer device that is capable of communicating across telephone lines to communicate with individuals who do not have such devices.

Remedies available to employees or job candidates who believe that their employment rights under the ADA have been violated are those specified under Title VII of the Civil Rights Act of 1964. Administrative enforcement by the Equal Employment Opportunity Commission is the first level of enforcement. The Equal Employment Opportunity Commission investigates the charge, and if "reasonable cause" is found for the charge, it attempts to mediate through informal means such as meetings. After administrative appeals have been exhausted, the right to sue in the federal courts is permitted. Employers violating the law are subject to fines, injunctions ordering compliance, and both back pay and future pay for the individuals who have proved discrimination. The enforcement is coordinated with the enforcement of the Rehabilitation Act of 1973 in order to prevent duplication of effort. The Equal Employment Opportunity Commission, the Attorney General, and the Office of Federal Contract Compliance Program have developed regulations to coordinate their enforcement authority.

Section 513 of the Americans with Disabilities Act encourages the use of Alternate Dispute Resolution (ADR) procedures in which the parties involved agree to follow specific guidelines in order to avoid costly, time-consuming legal action. ADR strategies include settlement negotiations, mediation, conciliation, facilitation, fact-finding, and arbitration. It is important to note that participation in conflict resolution procedures may not suspend time limits set for commencing administrative or court action.

Agencies charged with formulating regulations and standards for enforcing the ADA include the United States Access Board, the Department of Transportation, the Equal Employment Opportunity Commission, the Federal Communications Commission, and the Attorney General.

Copies of the ADA are available from Senators and Representatives and in public libraries. Regulations for enforcing individual sections of the act are available from the federal agencies charged with developing them and in the "Federal Register" (see "PUBLICATIONS" section below). In addition, many private agencies that work with individuals with disabilities have copies of the ADA available for distribution to the public.

Several court rulings have affected the implementation of the ADA. In 1999, the Supreme Court ruled in Olmstead, Commissioner, Georgia Department of Human Resources, et al. v. L.C. et al. that the ADA requires community placement instead of institutionalization whenever possible. The case was brought by two women who were both mentally retarded and mentally ill. Both had lived in state mental institutions for many years. Now their mental health professionals were recommending that they be placed in community-based treatment, but the state refused, saying it was more cost effective to keep the women hospitalized. The Supreme Court rejected the state's argument, citing Congress's intent that isolation and segregation were discrimination per se, and returned the case to the lower level court to determine appropriate relief. As a result of the Olmstead ruling, governments must place individuals in the community settings rather than in institutions whenever possible. This includes elders, who are often placed in nursing homes even though supplemental in-home services could allow them to remain in their own homes.

Two additional Supreme Court rulings in 1999 affected the definition of a disability under the ADA. In both Sutton v. United Airlines, Inc. and Murphy v. United Parcel Service, Inc., the Court ruled that when determining whether a disability is an ADA disability, an employer must consider whether the individual is using a "mitigating device" which enables the person to perform a major life activity with little or no difficulty. If the answer is yes, then the person is not protected by the ADA.

In 2002, the Supreme Court unanimously ruled that the ADA does not protect individuals with impairments that prevent them from carrying out manual tasks related to their jobs. In the case of Toyota Motor Manufacturing of Kentucky v. Williams, the Court said that workers must show that an impairment has substantial effect beyond the workplace in order to be covered by the ADA.

The *Rehabilitation Act of 1973* (P.L. 93-112) and its amendments have a variety of provisions that affect both private and public employers. States must submit a vocational rehabilitation plan to the Rehabilitation Services Administration (RSA) indicating how the designated state agency will provide vocational training, counseling, and diagnostic and evaluation services required by the law. The federal government provides funding to the states to carry out these services, and the Rehabilitation Services Administration, which is responsible for administering the Act, submits an annual report to the President with data on the number of clients served and cases closed.

Subsequent reauthorizations of and amendments to the Rehabilitation Act expanded the services provided under this law. For example, the "Client Assistance Program" (CAP) authorizes states to inform clients and other persons with disabilities about all available benefits under the Act and to assist them in obtaining all remedies due under the law (P.L. 98-221). CAP provides information about services and benefits under Title I of the Americans with Disabilities Act and advocates for services which facilitate employment.

The *Rehabilitation Act Amendments of 1992* (P.L. 102-569) establish state rehabilitation advisory councils composed of representatives of independent living councils, parents of children with disabilities, vocational rehabilitation professionals, and business; the role of these councils is to advise state vocational rehabilitation agencies and to prepare an annual report for the governor. The Amendments also establish a National Commission on Rehabilitation Services to study the quality and adequacy of rehabilitation services provided by the states. The *Rehabilitation Act Amendments of 1998* (P.L. 105-220, part of the Workforce Investment Act) aims to bring more Americans with disabilities into the mainstream workforce, The *Workforce Investment Act* (WIA) (P.L. 105-220) also established One-Stop Career Centers, which provide a full range of services to job seekers and must be accessible to people with disabilities.

Section 501 of the Rehabilitation Act prohibits federal agencies such as executive branch agencies and the Postal Service from discriminating against qualified individuals with disabilities. To assist federal agencies with this mandate, the Equal Employment Opportunity Commission has established affirmative action programs for the hiring and advancement of individuals with disabilities and guidelines for employment of individuals with disabilities. The Interagency Committee on Handicapped Employees is composed of representatives of executive agencies, the General Services Administration, and the Postal Service. The goals of the Committee are to increase employment of individuals with disabilities within the federal government and to provide a suitable work environment. Section 501 is enforced by the Equal Employment Opportunities Commission. Individuals who believe that they have been discriminated against must contact an equal employment opportunity counselor at the agency where the alleged discrimination took place. Individuals may also file a private lawsuit in U.S. district court within specified time periods.

Section 508 of the *Workforce Investment Act of 1998* (which includes the Rehabilitation Act Amendments of 1998) requires that the federal government provide access to electronic and information technology for all individuals with disabilities who are federal employees or who are members of the public seeking information or services from federal agencies. This includes making web sites accessible. If a federal agency claims that procurement of accessible technology poses an "undue burden," it must ensure that access to information is provided through alternative means. The United States Access Board has developed standards and guidelines for implementation of this mandate (See "ORGANIZATIONS" section below).

Section 503 of the Rehabilitation Act requires any contractor that receives more than $10,000 in contracts from the federal government to take affirmative action to employ individuals with disabilities. The employer's contract with the federal government must include a clause that states the contractor will take affirmative action to hire individuals with disabilities. This includes outreach efforts to hire employees with disabilities as well as reasonable accommodations for employees. Individuals who feel that contractors have violated the requirements of this section of the law may file a complaint with the U.S. Department of Labor. The Office of Federal Contract Compliance Programs within the U.S. Department of Labor is responsible for enforcing this provision (see "ORGANIZATIONS" section below). In order to carry out this function, the Office of Federal Contract Compliance Programs carries out compliance reviews, provides technical assistance to contractors to help them understand federal regulations, and investigates complaints.

Section 504 of the Rehabilitation Act prohibits any program that receives federal financial assistance from discriminating against individuals with disabilities who are otherwise eligible to benefit from their programs. Virtually all educational institutions are affected by this law, including private postsecondary institutions which receive federal financial assistance under a wide variety of programs. Programs must be physically accessible to individuals with disabilities, and construction begun after implementation of the regulations (June 3, 1977) must be designed so that it is in compliance with standard specifications for accessibility. Federal agencies must have an affirmative action plan for hiring, placing, and promoting individuals with disabilities and for making their facilities accessible. The Civil Rights Division of the Department of Justice is responsible for enforcing this section. Complainants need not exhaust administrative procedures but may file suit in federal district court against private employers who receive federal financial assistance, without filing complaints with the administrative agency.

Title VI of the Rehabilitation Act establishes "Employment Opportunities for Individuals with Disabilities." This section authorizes the federal government to establish pilot programs for community employment of individuals with disabilities. The "Projects with Industry" (PWI) authorizes the federal government to fund programs that enable individuals with disabilities to participate in the competitive labor market. Projects funded by the federal government work cooperatively with state vocational rehabilitation agencies and private employers. They provide job training, job placement, job and facility modification, and necessary technology. Individuals must be classified disabled by the state vocational rehabilitation agency in order to be eligible for services from Projects with Industry.

Section 402 of the *Vietnam Veterans Readjustment Assistance Act of 1974*, as amended, provides protection to veterans with disabilities as well as veterans of the Vietnam era. Contractors and subcontractors who have federal contracts for at least $10,000 annually must take affirmative action to employ, advance in employment, and otherwise treat covered veterans without discrimination. Section 402 is enforced by the U.S. Department of Labor, Office of Federal Contract Compliance Programs. Veterans may initiate complaints through their local veterans employment representative or designee at a local state employment office.

The *Health Insurance Portability and Accountability Act of 1996* (P.L. 104-191), also known as the Kennedy-Kassebaum law, protects individuals from being denied health insurance due to a pre-existing medical condition when they move from one job to another or if they become unemployed. "Portability" means that once individuals have been covered by health insurance, they are credited with having medical coverage when they enter a new plan. Group health plans, health insurance plans such as HMOs, Medicare, Medicaid, military health plans, Indian Health Service medical care, and public, state, or federal health benefits are considered creditable coverage (Fuch et al.: 1997). Coverage of a pre-existing medical condition may not be limited for more than 12 months for individuals who enroll in the health plan as soon as they are eligible (18 months for those who delay enrollment). Although the Act creates federal standards, the states have considerable flexibility in their requirements for insurers. The Departments of Treasury, Health and Human Services, and Labor are responsible for enforcing the provisions of the Act.

The *Family and Medical Leave Act of 1993* (P.L.103-3) requires employers with 50 or more employees at a worksite or within 75 miles of a worksite to permit eligible employees 12 workweeks of unpaid leave during a 12 month period in order to care for themselves, a spouse, son or daughter, or parent who has a serious health condition. During this period of leave, the employer must continue to provide group health benefits for the employee under the same conditions as the employee would have received while working. Upon return from leave, the employee must be restored to the same position he or she had prior to the leave or to a position with equivalent pay, benefits, and conditions of employment. Special regulations apply to employees of school systems and private schools and employees of the federal civil service.

The *Technology-Related Assistance for Individuals with Disabilities Act Amendments of 1994* (P.L. 103-218) strengthens the original Act, passed in 1988. The Act mandates state-wide programs for technology-related assistance to determine needs and resources; to provide technical assistance and information; and to develop demonstration and innovation projects, training programs, and public awareness programs. The amendments set priorities for consumer responsiveness, advocacy, systems change, and outreach to underrepresented populations such as the poor, individuals in rural areas, and minorities.

The *Architectural Barriers Act of 1968* (P.L. 90-480) required that all buildings and facilities constructed, altered, or leased with federal funds be accessible to individuals with disabilities. Five years after the Act was passed, under the authority of the Rehabilitation Act of 1973 (P.L. 93-112), the Architectural and Transportation Barriers Compliance Board (now the United States Access Board) was established to ensure compliance with the law and to provide assistance to local, state, and federal agencies in reaching their goal of eliminating barriers. (see Chapter 3, "Environmental Adaptations")

The *Telecommunications Act of 1996* (P.L. 104-104) has several sections that apply to individuals with disabilities. Section 254 redefines "universal service" to include schools, health facilities, and libraries and requires that the Federal Communications Commission (FCC) work with state governments to determine what services must be made universally available and what is considered "affordable." Section 255 requires that telecommunication equipment manufacturers and service providers be accessible to all individuals with disabilities, "if readily achievable." Section 713 requires that video services be accessible to individuals with hearing impairments via closed captioning and to individuals with visual impairments via descriptive video services. Section 706 requires that the FCC encourage the development of advanced telecommunications technology that provides equal access for individuals with disabilities, especially school children. The FCC is authorized to establish regulations and time tables for implementing these sections.

All states and many local governments have adopted their own laws regarding accessibility. Information about these laws may be obtained from the state or local office serving people with disabilities. In many areas, special legal services for people with disabilities are available, often with fees on a sliding scale. Check with the local bar association or with a law school. Some lawyers specialize in the legal needs of people with disabilities.

It is possible to locate the text of federal laws and information about federal programs on many sites on the Internet. The Library of Congress provides information on the status of proposed legislation, Congressional reports, and how to contact members of Congress at thomas.loc.gov.

FINANCIAL INCENTIVES

Under special programs administered by the Social Security Administration, it is possible for individuals with disabilities who receive cash benefits and health insurance from the federal government to work while receiving these benefits. The "PASS" program, or Plan to Achieve Self Support, provides incentives for people with disabilities to return to work. It allows recipients of Supplemental Security Income (SSI) to set aside income and resources for a specific time period while working to achieve an employment oriented goal. These goals may include education, starting a business, or obtaining assistive technology. Income set aside under the PASS program is not counted in the SSI income and resources tests. In the "Trial

Work Period" program, recipients of Social Security Disability Insurance (SSDI) may work for up to nine months in a five year period during which they earn more than the substantial gainful activity level without affecting benefits. Months in which earnings do not exceed the substantial gainful activity level are not counted toward the trial work period. After completion of nine months with substantial gainful activity, individuals may receive benefits during a three year extended period for any month in which their earnings are not at the substantial gainful activity level. The cost of "Impairment-Related Work Expenses" may be deducted when calculating income for eligibility for Supplemental Security Income or Social Security Disability Insurance. The Social Security Administration provides information on these programs through its toll-free number [(800) 772-1213 or (800) 325-0778 (TTY)] or at local Social Security offices (ask for the work incentives specialist).

The *Ticket to Work and Work Incentives Improvement Act of 1999* (P.L. 106-170) created a program, sponsored by the Social Security Administration; it mails out tickets to work to individuals with disabilities, who take them to participating agencies in the employment network that help them design and implement an employment plan. Individuals who find employment through this program maintain their Medicare or Medicaid health insurance. It also created new options and incentives for states to offer a Medicaid buy-in for workers with disabilities and extends Medicare coverage for an additional four and one-half years for people on disability who return to work.

Under Section 190 of the *Tax Reform Act of 1986*, qualified business owners may deduct qualified expenses for business expenses including disability related expenditures and medical expenses. These include wheelchairs, text telephones, and the like. Additional deductions include the cost of removing architectural and transportation barriers. Section 44 of the *Omnibus Budget Reconciliation Act of 1990* allows eligible small businesses a tax credit for eligible access expenditures. Work Opportunity Tax Credits provide employers with tax credits for hiring members of certain targeted low-income groups, including individuals with disabilities who are referred by state vocational rehabilitation agencies or the Department of Veterans Affairs. Contact the Internal Revenue Service to obtain publications that explain these benefits.

References

Fuch, Beth C. et al.
1997   The Health Insurance Portability and Accountability Act of 1996: Guidance
        Washington DC: Library of Congress, Congressional Research Service
Kaye, H. Stephen
1998   Is the Status of People with Disabilities Improving? Abstract # 21 May Disability
        Statistics Center, University of California, San Francisco40

ORGANIZATIONS

Civil Rights Center
U.S. Department of Labor
200 Constitution Avenue, NW, Room 4123
Washington, DC 20210
(202) 693-6501   (800)326-2577 (TTY)
FAX (202) 693-7888   lockhart.annabelle@dol.gov   www.dol.gov

This office enforces the Workforce Investment Act to ensure that recipients of federal funding from this act do not discriminate against people with disabilities. A "Checklist" has been developed to ensure that uniform procedures are used to investigate compliance with the law.

Client Assistance Program (CAP)
Rehabilitation Services Administration
U.S. Department of Education
400 Maryland Avenue, SW, Room 3225
Washington, DC 20202-2500
(202) 205-8719   FAX (202) 205-9340
roseann.ashby@ed.gov   www.ed.gov/programs/rsacap

Established by the Rehabilitation Act of 1973, as amended, CAP provides information and advocacy for individuals with disabilities served under the Act and Title I of the Americans with Disabilities Act. Assistance is also provided to facilitate employment.

Commission on Mental and Physical Disability Law
American Bar Association
740 15th Street, NW, 9th Floor
Washington, DC 20005-1009
(202) 662-1570   (202) 662-1012 (TTY)   FAX (202) 662-1032
cmpdl@abanet.org   www.abanet.org/disability

Operates a Disability Legal Support Center, which provides searches of databases of laws, legal cases, and recent developments in the field of disability. Provides technical consultations on rights, enforcement, and other issues related to the Americans with Disabilities Act. Web site has a directory of lawyers who specialize in disability law.

Cornell University Program on Employment and Disability
New York State School of Industrial and Labor Relations, Extension Division
106 ILR Extension Building
Ithaca, NY 14853
(607) 255-7797   (607) 255-2891 (TTY)   FAX (607) 255-2763
ilru_ped@cornell.edu   www.ilr.cornell.edu/ped

This program seeks to improve employment practices covered by Title I of the Americans with Disabilities Act. Produces and disseminates publications on Title I, transition from school to work, and supported employment. Catalogue available on the web site. Conducts research, provides technical assistance, and conducts training programs for employers throughout the U.S. and abroad.

Disability Rights Education and Defense Fund (DREDF)
2212 6th Street
Berkeley, CA 94710
(510) 644-2555 (V/TTY)   FAX (510) 841-8645   dredf@dredf.org
www.dredf.org

Provides technical assistance, information, and referrals on laws and rights; provides legal representation to people with disabilities in both individual and class action cases; trains law students, parents, and legislators. ADA Hotline [(800)-466-4232 (V/TTY)] provides information on the Americans with Disabilities Act. Quarterly newsletter, "Disability Rights News," available in standard print, alternate formats, and on the web site. Free

Disability Rights Section
Civil Rights Division
U.S. Department of Justice
950 Pennsylvania Avenue, NW
Washington, DC 205308
(800) 514-0301   (800) 514-0383 (TTY)
FAX (202) 307-1198   ada.gov

Responsible for enforcing Titles II and III of the Americans with Disabilities Act. Copies of its regulations are available in standard print, alternate formats, audiocassette, disk, and braille and on the web site. Callers may request publications, obtain technical assistance, and speak to an ADA specialist. Many publications available through fax-on-demand system. The ADA Business Connection provides information to help business owners understand their legal obligations and their rights (www.ada.gov/business.htm). The web site has many publications on tax credits.

Equal Employment Opportunity Commission (EEOC)
1801 L Street, NW, 10th Floor
Washington, DC 20507
(800) 669-3362 to order publications
(800) 669-4000 to speak to an investigator
(800) 800-6820 (TTY)
In the Washington, DC metropolitan area, (202) 663-4900
(202) 663-4494 (TTY)   www.eeoc.gov

Responsible for promulgating and enforcing regulations for the employment section of the ADA. Fifty-one field offices throughout the U.S. Copies of its regulations are available in standard print and alternate formats. Many publications available on the web site.

Federal Communications Commission (FCC)
445 12th Street, SW
Washington, DC 20554
(888) 225-5322   (888) 835-5322 (TTY)   (202) 418-0190
(202) 418-2555 (TTY)   www.fcc.gov

Responsible for developing regulations for telecommunication issues related to federal laws, including the Americans with Disabilities Act and the Telecommunications Act of 1996.

Internal Revenue Service (IRS)
(800) 829-3676 to order forms   (800) 829-1040 for general information
(800) 829-4059 (TTY)
(202) 622-3110 information for business requirements under the ADA
www.irs.gov

Provides information and publications about tax deductions for businesses that make accommodations for employees with disabilities and about the Work Opportunity Tax Credit Program.

Justice for All
www.jfanow.org

This web site provides alerts regarding Congressional actions on issues related to disabilities. Web site provides instructions for signing up for alerts.

National Council on Disability (NCD)
1331 F Street, NW, Suite 850
Washington, DC 20004-1107
(202) 272-2004   (202) 272-2074 (TTY)   FAX (202) 272-2022
mquigley@ncd.gov   www.ncd.gov

An independent federal agency mandated to study and make recommendations about public policy for people with disabilities. Holds regular meetings and hearings in various locations around the country. Publishes monthly newsletter, "NCD Bulletin," available in standard print, alternate formats, and via e-mail. Free

Office for Civil Rights
U.S. Department of Health and Human Services
200 Independence Avenue, SW
Washington, DC 20201
(202) 619-0700   (202) 863-0101 (TTY)   FAX (202) 619-3818
www.hhs.gov/progorg/ocrhmpg.html

Responsible for enforcing laws and regulations that protect the rights of individuals seeking medical and social services in institutions that receive federal financial assistance. Individuals who feel their rights have been violated may file a complaint with one of the ten regional offices located throughout the country.

Office of Civil Rights
Federal Transit Administration
400 7th Street, NW
Washington, DC 20590
(888) 446-4511   (202) 366-4018   (202) 366-0153 (TTY)
ada.assistance@fta.dot.gov   www.fta.dot.gov

Responsible for investigating complaints covered by mandates set forth in the Americans with Disabilities Act regarding the transportation of individuals with disabilities. Web site provides complaint form.

Office of Civil Rights
U.S. Department of Education
300 C Street, SW
Washington, DC 20202
(800) 421-3481   (877) 521-2172 (TTY)   (202) 205-5413
FAX (202) 205-9862   OCR@ed.gov
www.ed.gov/about/offices/list/ocr/index.html

*Responsible for enforcing laws and regulations designed to protect the rights of individuals in educational institutions that receive federal financial assistance. Individuals who feel their rights have been violated may file a complaint with one of the ten regional offices located throughout the country.

Office of Federal Contract Compliance Programs (OFCCP)
Employment Standards Administration
U.S. Department of Labor
200 Constitution Avenue, NW, Room C-3325
Washington, DC 20210
(888) 378-3227   (202) 219-9475   FAX (202) 219-6195
www.dol.gov/dol/esa/ofccp/index.htm

Reviews contractors' affirmative action plans; provides technical assistance to contractors; investigates complaints; and resolves issues between contractors and employees. Ten regional offices throughout the country serve as liaisons with the national office and with district offices under their jurisdiction.
regulations and complaint forms.

Office of General Counsel
U.S. Department of Transportation
400 7th Street, SW
Washington, DC 20590
(202) 366-9306   (202) 755-7687 (TTY)   FAX (202) 366-9313
www.dot.gov

Responsible for providing information and interpretation of the regulations for transportation of individuals with disabilities required by the Rehabilitation Act and the Americans with Disabilities Act. Regulations available in standard print or on audiocassette.

Rehabilitation Services Administration (RSA)
U.S. Department of Education
400 Maryland Avenue, SW, Room 3329-MES
Washington, DC 20202-2251
(202) 205-5482   FAX (202) 205-9874
www.ed.gov/about/offices/list/osers/osers/about.html

The principal federal agency mandated to carry out the provisions of the Rehabilitation Act of 1973 and its amendments.

Social Security Administration (SSA)
6401 Security Boulevard
Baltimore, MD 21235
(800) 772-1213   (800) 325-0778 (TTY)
www.socialsecurity.gov

Special rules enable people with disabilities who receive Supplemental Security Income (SSI) or Social Security Disability Insurance (SSDI) to continue receiving these benefits and Medicare or Medicaid while they are working. Call the number listed above and ask for the work incentives expert in order to learn about the rules for these programs.

Thomas
Library of Congress
thomas.loc.gov

This online service provides a database of recent laws and pending legislation, as well as information about the committees of Congress and the text of the "Congressional Record." Searches for legislation and laws may be done by topic or public law number.

Ticket to Work
Maximus
11419 Sunset Hill Road
Reston, VA 20190
(866) 968-7842   www.yourtickettowork.com

This program, sponsored by the Social Security Administration, mails out tickets to work to individuals with disabilities, who take them to participating agencies in the employment network that help them design and implement an employment plan. Individuals who find employment through this program maintain their Medicare or Medicaid health insurance.

United States Access Board
1331 F Street, NW, Suite 1000
Washington, DC 20004-1111
(800) 872-2253   (800) 993-2822 (TTY)   (202) 272-5434
(202) 272-5449 (TTY)   FAX (202) 272-5447
info@access-board.gov   www.access-board.gov

A federal agency charged with developing standards for accessibility in federal facilities, public accommodations, and transportation facilities as required by the Americans with Disabilities Act and other federal laws. Publishes the "Uniform Federal Accessibility Standards," which describes accessibility standards for buildings and dwelling units developed for four federal agencies. Provides technical assistance, sponsors research, and distributes publications. Developed standards for Section 508 requirements for electronic and information technology. Guidelines available on the web site (www.access-board.gov/508.htm). Publishes free bimonthly newsletter, "Access Currents," available in standard print, alternate formats, via e-mail, and on the web site.

PUBLICATIONS

ADA Document Portal
U.S. Department of Education
www.adaportal.org

This web site includes thousands of documents related to the Americans with Disabilities Act. Includes documents related to employment.

ADA Job Accommodations Analysis Worksheet
Elliott and Fitzpatrick
1135 Cedar Shoals Drive
Athens, GA 30605
(800) 843-4977   FAX (706) 227-2204
orders@elliottfitzpatrick.com   www.elliottfitzpatrick.com

This worksheet enables employer and applicant to analyze a job for required or helpful accommodations. Package of 50, $ 18.00.

Americans with Disabilities Act Fact Sheet
United States Access Board
1331 F Street, NW, Suite 1000
Washington, DC 20004-1111
(800) 872-2253   (800) 993-2822 (TTY)   (202) 272-5434
(202) 272-5449 (TTY)   FAX (202) 272-5447
info@access-board.gov   www.access-board.gov

This fact sheet provides an overview of the Americans with Disabilities Act's major titles, requirements, and effective dates. Presented in table format. Available in standard print, large print, braille, audiocassette, and disk. Also available on the web site. Free

Americans with Disabilities Act Manual and Newsletter
Bureau of National Affairs
1231 25th Street, NW
Washington, DC 20037
(800) 372-1033   customercare@bna.com   www.bna.com

This manual and bimonthly newsletter follows current court decisions and monitors federal and state legislation and regulations. Manual and newsletter, $657.00; newsletter only, $266.00

The Americans with Disabilities Act: Questions and Answers
The Americans with Disabilities Act: Your Employment Rights as an Individual
The Americans with Disabilities Act: Your Responsibility as an Employer
Equal Employment Opportunity Commission (EEOC)
1801 L Street, NW, 10th Floor
Washington, DC 20507
(800) 669-3362 to order publications
(800) 669-4000 to speak to an investigator
(800) 800-6820 (TTY)
In the Washington, DC metropolitan area, (202) 663-4900
(202) 663-4494 (TTY)   www.eeoc.gov

These brochures discuss the most common questions concerning the Americans with Disabilities Act in general and what employees and employers need to know. Free. Also available on the web site.

The Appeals Process
Compilation of Social Security Laws
Disability Benefits: The Social Security Handbook
How to File an Unfair Treatment Complaint
Supplemental Security Income Programs (SSI)
Ticket to Work and Self-Sufficiency Programs
Your Right to Question the Decision Made on Your Claim
Your Right to Question the Decision Made on Your SSI Claim
Social Security Administration
(800) 772-1213   (800) 325-0778 (TTY)   www.socialsecurity.gov

These booklets provide basic information about Social Security programs for individuals with disabilities. The Social Security Administration distributes many other titles, including many that are available in large print, braille, and audiocassette. Publications are available on the web site and at local Social Security offices. Free

Directory of Legal Aid and Defender Offices
National Legal Aid and Defender Association
1140 Connecticut Avenue, NW, Suite 900
Washington, DC 20036
(202) 452-0620   FAX (202) 872-1031   info@nlada.org
www.nlada.org

A directory of legal aid offices throughout the U.S. Includes chapters on disability protection/advocacy, health law, and senior citizens. Updated biennially. $90.00

Disability Law Compliance Report
West Group
PO Box 64833
St. Paul, MN 55264-0833
(800) 328-4880   FAX (800) 340-9378
west.customer.service@thoson.com www.westgroup.com

A monthly newsletter that reviews case law and agency decisions related to the Americans with Disabilities Act. $314.00

The Disability Rights Movement: From Charity to Confrontation
by Doris Zames Fleischer and Frieda Zames
Temple University Press
c/o Chicago Distribution Center
11030 South Langley Avenue
Chicago, IL 60628
(800) 621-2736   (215) 204-8787
FAX (800) 621-8476   tempress@astro.mail.temple.edu
www.temple.edu/tempress

This book presents the history of the disability rights movement in the U.S. It discusses deinstitutionalization and independent living, legislation, education, and technology. Includes the Americans with Disabilities Act and Section 504 of the Civil Rights Act. Hardcover, $79.59; softcover, $24.95.

EEOC Enforcement Guidelines: Reasonable Accommodations and Undue Hardship under the Americans with Disabilities Act (ADA)
Equal Employment Opportunities Distribution Center
1801 L Street, NW, 10th Floor
Washington, DC 20507
(800) 669-3362 to order publications
(800) 669-4000 to speak to an investigator
(800) 800-68203302 (TTY)In the Washington, DC metropolitan area, (202) 663-4900
(202) 663-4494 (TTY)   www.eeoc.gov

This policy statement discusses the requirement that employers provide "reasonable accommodation" to job applicants and employees with disabilities under Title I of the Americans with Disabilities Act and answers many frequently asked questions. Free. Also available on the web site.

Federal Register
New Orders, Superintendent of Documents
PO Box 371954
Pittsburgh, PA 15250-7954
(866) 512-1800   FAX (202) 512-2250
gpoaccess@gpo.gov   bookstore.gpo.gov

A federal publication printed every weekday with notices of all regulations and legal notices issued by federal agencies. Domestic subscriptions, $764.00 annually. Also available on the web site at no charge.

Filing a Charge of Job Discrimination
Equal Employment Opportunity Commission (EEOC)
1801 L Street, NW, 10th Floor
Washington, DC 20507
(800) 669-3362 to order publications
(800) 669-4000 to speak to an investigator
(800) 800-68203302 (TTY)
In the Washington, DC metropolitan area, (202) 663-4900
(202) 663-4494 (TTY)   www.eeoc.gov

This brochure describes what laws are applicable for charges of job discrimination, which types of employers are covered, the procedures for filing a complaint, and the remedies that are available.

From Good Will to Civil Rights
by Richard K. Scotch
Temple University Press
c/o Chicago Distribution Center
11030 South Langley Avenue
Chicago, IL 60628
(800) 621-2736   FAX (800) 621-8476
kh@press.uchicago.edu   www.press.chicago.edu

Based on interviews conducted with individuals who worked behind the scenes, including members of the disability rights movement, this book describes the history of Section 504 of the Rehabilitation Act. It discusses changes in federal disability policy that resulted from the Rehabilitation Act and the Americans with Disabilities Act. Hardcover, $59.50; softcover, $18.95.

A Guide for People with Disabilities Seeking Employment
Civil Rights Division
U.S. Department of Justice
950 Pennsylvania Avenue, NW
Washington, DC 205308
(800) 514-0301   (800) 514-0383 (TTY)
FAX (202) 307-1198   ada.gov

This booklet discusses reasonable accommodations, how to obtain them, and how to file a complaint. Free. Also available on the web site.

A Guide to Disability Rights Laws
Disability Rights Section, Civil Rights Division
U.S. Department of Justice
PO Box 66738
Washington, DC 20035-6738
(800) 514-0301   (800) 514-0383 (TTY)
(202) 514-0301   (202) 514-0383 (TTY)
www.usdoj.gov/crt/ada/adahom1.htm

This booklet provides an overview of the Americans with Disabilities Act, Fair Housing Act, Air Carrier Access Act, Civil Rights of Institutionalized Persons Act, Individuals with Disabilities Education Act, Rehabilitation Act, and the Architectural Barriers Act. Available in standard print, large print, audiocassette, braille, disk, and on the web site. Free

Guide to the Family and Medical Leave Act
The National Partnership for Women and Families
National Partnership for Women and Families
1875 Connecticut Avenue, NW, Suite 650
Washington, DC 20009
(202) 986-2600   FAX (202) 986-2539
info@nationalpartnership.org www.nationalpartnership.org

This booklet answers the most frequently asked questions about the law. Available in English and Spanish. Free. Also available on the web site.

Health Benefits Under COBRA
Federal Citizens Information Center
PO Box 100
Pueblo, CO 81002
(888) 878-3256   FAX (719) 948-9724
cic.info@pueblo.gsa.gov   www.pueblo.gsa.gov

This booklet describes the coverage provided by the Consolidated Omnibus Budget Reconciliation Act (COBRA). $.50 Also available on the web site.

Health Insurance Resource Manual: Options for People with a Chronic Disease or Disability
by Dorothy E. Northrop and Stephen Cooper
Demos Medical Publishing
386 Park Avenue South, Suite 201
New York, NY 10016
(800) 532-8663   (212) 683-0072   FAX (212) 683-0118
info@demospub.com   www.demosmedpub.com

This book provides an overview of health insurance plans; government programs such as Social Security, Medicare, Medicaid, and the federal laws that affect health insurance; and resources for conducting research on health insurance options. $24.95. Orders placed on the Demos web site receive a 15% discount.

Insurance Solutions--Plan Well, Live Better: A Workbook for People with Chronic Illnesses or Disabilities
by Laura D. Cooper
Demos Medical Publishing
386 Park Avenue South, Suite 201
New York, NY 10016
(800) 532-8663   (212) 683-0072   FAX (212) 683-0118
info@demospub.com   www.demosmedpub.com

This book enables readers to find and evaluate insurance options. Includes checklists, worksheets, and exercises. $24.95. Orders placed on the Demos web site receive a 15% discount.

Medicare & You
Centers for Medicare and Medicaid Services (CMS)
formerly Health Care Financing Administration (HCFA)
7500 Security Boulevard
Baltimore, MD 21244
(877) 267-2323   (866) 226-1819 (TTY)   (410) 786-3000
www.medicare.gov

This booklet provides basic information about Medicare including eligibility, enrollment, coverage, and options. Available in English and Spanish in standard print and alternate formats. Free. Also available on the web site.

Mental and Physical Disability Law Reporter
Commission on Mental and Physical Disability Law
American Bar Association
740 15th Street, NW, 9th Floor
Washington, DC 20005-1009
(202) 662-1581   (202) 662-1012 (TTY)   FAX (202) 662-1032
cmpdl@abanet.org   www.abanet.org/disability

A bimonthly journal with court decisions, legislative and regulatory news, and articles on treatment, accessibility, employment, education, federal programs, etc. Individual subscription, $314.00; organizational subscription, $374.00. Reprints of articles from back issues available.

Rehabilitating Section 504
National Council on Disability (NCD)
1331 F Street, NW, Suite 850
Washington, DC 20004-1107
(202) 272-2004   (202) 272-2074 (TTY)   FAX (202) 272-2022
mquigley@ncd.gov   www.ncd.gov

This report analyzes the compliance and federal enforcement of this law and suggests ways to improve its shortcomings. Available on the web site. Free

Report on Disability Programs
Business Publishers
8737 Colesville Road, Suite 1100
Silver Spring, MD 20910-3928
(800) 274-6737   (301) 589-5103
FAX (301) 589-8493   bpinews@bpinews.com   www.bpinews.com

A biweekly newsletter with information on policies promulgated by federal agencies, laws, and funding sources. Print version, $327.00; e-mail version $277.00

Section 504 Compliance Handbook
Thompson Publishing Group
1725 K Street, NW, Suite 700
Washington, DC 20006
(800) 964-5815   (813) 282-8807   service@thompson.com
www.thompson.com

A reference book and monthly updates that describe rules made by federal agencies and analyze case law related to Section 504 of the Rehabilitation Act, applicable to organizations that receive federal contracts. $327.00

A Summary of Department of Veterans Affairs Benefits
(800) 827-1000   www.va.gov

This booklet is available from any VA regional office.   Free

A Technical Assistance Manual on the Employment Provisions of Title I of the Americans with Disabilities Act
Equal Employment Opportunity Commission (EEOC)
1801 L Street, NW, 10th Floor
Washington, DC 20507
(800) 669-3362 to order publications
(800) 669-4000 to speak to an investigator
(800) 800-6820TTY)
In the Washington, DC metropolitan area, (202) 663-4900
(202) 663-4494 (TTY)   www.eeoc.gov

Provides an overview of the legal requirements, information about qualified individuals with disabilities, reasonable accommodations, hiring, medical examinations, workers' compensation, enforcement of the law, and a resource directory that includes regional and state locations of enforcement offices.   Free

Telecommunications Act Accessibility Guidelines
United States Access Board
1331 F Street, NW, Suite 1000
Washington, DC 20004-1111
(800) 872-2253   (800) 993-2822 (TTY)   (202) 272-5434
(202) 272-5449 (TTY)   FAX (202) 272-5447
info@access-board.gov   www.access-board.gov

These final guidelines cover access to telecommunications under the Telecommunications Act of 1996. Free. Also available in large print, braille, audiocassette, disk, and on the web site.

Chapter 3

ENVIRONMENTAL ADAPTATIONS

Many of the adaptations that enable employees with disabilities to work comfortably and safely are easy to achieve. Several studies have shown that most workplace accommodations are either inexpensive or cost nothing at all. For example, swing-clear hinges installed in place of conventional hinges add one and a half to two inches to the open width of a door. This extra width may provide access for wheelchair users. Special levers may be installed over standard door knobs to help individuals with limited hand function to open doors easily. Paper towel dispensers installed at a lower than usual level, hand rails, and faucet levers instead of knobs are easily installed in the workplace. Anti-fatigue floor mats and slanted foot rests can make some work stations more comfortable and relieve stress on workers' feet and lower backs. Laboratory equipment and other furniture can be lowered to a height that is accessible to employees who use wheelchairs.

Application of the concept of "universal design" in designing new facilities, furniture, and equipment will make life easier for all individuals, including those with disabilities. "Universal design" means that design of buildings and products will accommodate the broadest potential population of users, including those with and those without disabilities. For example, wide entryways without thresholds will not only enable wheelchair users to have access, but they will also be safer and easier to use for individuals who do not use wheelchairs. Large print on the screens of computer monitors will not only enable individuals with visual impairments access to the screen but will also be easier to read for individuals without visual impairments. Incorporating these adaptations into the general marketplace also reduces the cost.

Business owners and property developers must be aware of accessibility standards when planning new construction or renovation of existing buildings. States and municipalities often have organizations that monitor architectural accessibility to ensure compliance with the required standards. Prior to making renovations or starting new construction, it is wise to obtain a copy of state and local laws as well as federal standards to be certain that the plans comply with all requirements. State architectural access boards may have a specific set of regulations pertaining to different types of construction, such as residences, hotels, hospitals, and schools, as well as site requirements. State chapters of the American Institute of Architects make referrals to members who specialize in barrier-free design.

Employees themselves are often the best resources for suggesting adaptations. An advisory committee made up of employees with disabilities can provide extremely important information to those who are designing renovations and new construction. In addition to suggesting general adaptations for the facility, employees themselves can indicate the types of adaptations they need to perform their own jobs. However, employees are usually not experts on government standards, which change with new legislation.

The Americans with Disabilities Act of 1990 (ADA) guarantees access to public accommodations and mandates the development of standards for design and construction of new facilities and alteration of existing facilities. The Americans with Disabilities Act

Accessibility Guidelines for Buildings and Facilities (ADAAG) were published by the Architectural and Transportation Barriers Compliance Board (now the United States Access Board) to guide the Department of Justice in establishing accessibility standards. At the time this book went to press, the United States Access Board had approved updates to the ADAAG rules and was awaiting approval from the Office of Management and Budget (OMB) prior to publishing them. Information about these rules may be found at www.access-board.gov/ada-aba/status.htn.

Newly constructed and altered places of public accommodation and commercial facilities, such as restaurants, hotels, and mercantile and business establishments, must use the ADAAG accessibility standards for the implementation of Title III of the ADA (Architectural and Transportation Barriers Compliance Board: 1992). Under Title II, state and local governments are given the option to choose between the ADAAG or the Uniform Federal Accessibility Standards (UFAS). However, an exemption regarding elevator requirements included in Title III of the ADA does not apply if the ADAAG is chosen.

The Uniform Federal Accessibility Standards are a set of design, construction, and alteration guidelines developed under the guidance of the Architectural and Transportation Barriers Compliance Board (now the United States Access Board) prior to the enactment of the Americans with Disabilities Act (General Services Administration et al.: 1988). These guidelines are also intended to be consistent with the standards of the American National Standards Institute (ANSI). ANSI is a private organization that has developed standards for barrier-free design through a committee that represents individuals with disabilities, rehabilitation professionals, designers, manufacturers, and builders. Both the Architectural Barriers Act of 1968 and Section 504 of the Rehabilitation Act of 1973 reference the UFAS guidelines in setting standards for state and local governments that receive federal funds.

Some of the ADAAG and UFAS technical specifications are identical, such as the requirements for accessible routes within buildings and connecting facilities and the width, passing space, changes in level, doors, and emergency exits from the buildings. ADAAG specifications are the same as UFAS standards for ramps, stairs, mirrors, sinks, storage, and a host of other elements and spaces.

The Department of Justice has indicated that it anticipates supplementing the ADAAG standards and applying them to state and local government facilities as well as facilities that have received federal financing. Consistent standards and uniform design are goals of the United States Access Board (formerly the Architectural and Transportation Barriers Compliance Board as it issues guidelines for the Department of Justice.

FINANCIAL INCENTIVES FOR ARCHITECTURAL BARRIER REMOVAL

Financial and tax benefits are available to businesses through the Tax Reform Act of 1986. Section 190 of this act offers all businesses a deduction for expenses incurred in removing barriers that prevent access for individuals with disabilities and elders. Instead of deducting these expenses as depreciation over many years, the taxpayer may deduct them in one year. Section 190 applies to architectural barriers such as grading levels, parking lots, accessible routes, ramps and curbs, doors and doorways, stairs and railings, floors, bathrooms and bathroom furnishings, elevators, telephones, and signs. Section 190 also allows deductions

55

for unspecified alterations as long as the removal of the barrier provides access to the facility or public transportation vehicle by individuals with disabilities or elders. The barriers that are removed must not create new barriers to access for any other group of individuals with disabilities. Deductions are also available for transportation systems, including rail facilities, buses, and rapid and light rail vehicles.

In addition to Section 190, under the Omnibus Budget Reconciliation Act of 1990, Section 44, eligible small businesses may receive a general business credit of fifty percent of the cost of making their buildings accessible for ADA compliance (with a maximum credit of $5,000). A small business is one that has less than one million dollars in gross receipts and employs fewer than 30 full-time employees (Architectural and Transportation Barriers Compliance Board: 1990). Fifty percent of eligible access expenditures that exceed $250 but do not exceed $10,250 per taxable year are covered. The access credit may apply to removal of architectural, transportation, or communications barriers; providing interpreters, readers, or other aids for employees who have hearing or vision impairments; and acquiring or modifying equipment for use by individuals with disabilities.

References

Architectural and Transportation Barriers Compliance Board
1992   "Americans with Disabilities Act (ADA) Accessibility Guidelines for Buildings and Facilities; State and Local Government Facilities" Federal Register 57:(December 21)245:60613
1990   "ADA Tax Credit" Access America Fall/Winter
General Services Administration, Department of Defense, Department of Housing and Urban Development, and U.S. Postal Service
1988   Uniform Federal Accessibility Standards Fed-Std-795, April 1

Center for Universal Design
North Carolina State University
Box 8613
Raleigh, NC 27695-8613
(800) 647-6777   (919) 515-3082 (V/TTY)
FAX (919) 515-7330   cud@ncsu.edu   www.design.ncsu.edu/cud

A federally funded research and training center that works toward improving housing and product design for people with disabilities. Provides technical assistance, training, and publications. Some publications are available on the web site.

Internal Revenue Service (IRS)
Office of The Chief Counsel
1111 Constitution Avenue, NW
Washington, DC 20224
(202) 622-3110   FAX (202) 622-4524
www.ustreas.gov/offices/general-counsel/chief-counsel/irs.html

Provides information and interpretation of Section 190 of the Tax Reform Act and Section 44 of the Omnibus Budget Reconciliation Act of 1990.

Job Accommodation Network (JAN)
West Virginia University
PO Box 6080
Morgantown, WV 26506-6080
(800) 526-7234 (V/TTY)   (800) 232-9675 (V/TTY)   (304) 293-7186 (V/TTY)
FAX (304) 293-5407   jan@jan.wvu.edu
www.jan.wvu.edu/links/adalinks.htm

Funded by the U.S. Department of Labor, JAN maintains database of products that facilitate accommodation in the workplace. Provides information to employers about practical accommodations which enable them to employ individuals with disabilities. Advises individuals and businesses about the Americans with Disabilities Act. The web site listed above covers laws, Supreme Court decisions, guidebooks, and other materials related to the Americans with Disabilities Act.

Rehabilitation Engineering Research Center on Universal Design
School of Architecture and Planning
State University of New York at Buffalo
Buffalo, NY 1214-3087
(800) 628-2281   (716) 829-3285 ext. 329
FAX (716) 829-3861   rercud@ap.buffalo.edu   www.ap.buffalo.edu/idea

This federally funded project conducts research on people who use both wheelchairs and scooters. Distributes a monthly E-Newsletter. Free

United States Access Board
1331 F Street, NW, Suite 1000
Washington, DC 20004-1111
(800) 872-2253   (800) 993-2822 (TTY)   (202) 272-5434
(202) 272-5449 (TTY)   FAX (202) 272-5447
info@access-board.gov   www.access-board.gov

A federal agency charged with developing standards for accessibility in federal facilities, public accommodations, and transportation facilities as required by the Americans with Disabilities Act and other federal laws. Publishes the "Uniform Federal Accessibility Standards," which describes accessibility standards for buildings and dwelling units developed for four federal agencies. Provides technical assistance, sponsors research, and distributes publications. Publishes quarterly newsletter, "Access America" and bimonthly newsletter, "Access Currents." Free. Publications available in standard print, large print, braille, audiocassette, disk, via e-mail and on the web site.

The ADA: Your Personal Guide to the Law
Tax Incentives: Assisting Accessibility
Paralyzed Veterans of America
801 18th Street, NW
Washington, DC 20006
(800) 424-8200   (800) 795-4327 (TTY)   (202) 872-1300
FAX (202) 785-4452   info@pva.org   www.pva.org
Publications Distribution Center: (888) 860-7244

These publications describe the tax incentives for removal of architectural barriers provided by Section 190 of the Tax Reform Act, the ADA, and Section 44 of the Omnibus Budget Reconciliation Act of 1990. Free. Also available on the web site.

Job Accommodation Handbook
RPM Press, Inc.
PO Box 31483
Tucson, AZ 85751
(888) 810-1990   FAX (520) 886-1990   pmccray@theriver.com
www.rpmpress.com

Discusses reasonable and low-cost accommodations, job restructuring, and job placements. Includes sample job analysis and accommodation forms. $39.95

Specifications for Making Buildings and Facilities Accessible to, and Usable by, Physically Handicapped People
Global Engineering
15 Inverness East
Glenwood, CO 80112
(800) 854-7179   FAX (314) 726-6418   www.global.ihs.com

Lists ANSI standards for barrier-free design. Order A117.1 - 1998. May be downloaded for web site, $26.00; print copy, $26.00

Teaching Chemistry to Students with Disabilities: A Manual for High School and College Students
Committee on Chemists with Disabilities
American Chemical Society (ACS)
1155 16th Street, NW
Washington, DC 20036
(800) 227-5558   (202) 872-4432 (V/TTY)   cwd@acs.org
www.acs.org

Although this booklet was written to enable teachers to make laboratory work accessible for students with mobility, hearing, or visual impairments, the information provided is useful for workplaces with scientific laboratories as well. Free. Also available on the web site at membership.acs.org/c/cwd/TeachChem4.pdf. The Committee on Chemists with Disabilities will also make referrals.

Uniform Federal Accessibility Standards (UFAS)
United States Access Board
1331 F Street, NW, Suite 1000
Washington, DC 20004-1111
(800) 872-2253   (800) 993-2822 (TTY)   (202) 272-5434
(202) 272-5449 (TTY)   FAX (202) 272-5447
info@access-board.gov   www.access-board.gov

Presents uniform minimum standards for use in designing, constructing, and altering buildings to provide access for individuals with disabilities in accordance with the Architectural Barriers Act of 1968 (P.L. 90-480) as amended through 1984. Available in print, on disk, and on the web site. Free

Uniform System for Handicapped Parking
Federal Register, Volume 56, Number 47, March 11, 1991 10327-10344
National Highway Safety Administration
Department of Transportation
400 Seventh Street, SW
Washington, DC 20590
(202) 366-1834   FAX (202) 366-3820

Contains regulations for a standard system of handicapped parking, including the use of placards and special licenses, and parking space design. May be downloaded from web site: www.access.gpo.gov (Federal Information at Your Fingertips)

Chapter 4

ASSISTIVE TECHNOLOGY

The dramatic increase in the variety of assistive devices has opened up a vast array of jobs for individuals with disabilities. While many people think of assistive technology as sophisticated "high tech" electronic equipment with a high price tag, many items are "low tech," simple adaptations to the work environment. For example, commonly used office equipment such as electric staplers, photocopiers which automatically collate documents, and electric letter openers enable individuals with arthritis to save energy and reduce stress on their joints.

It is often cost-effective to examine low tech alternatives before turning to complex devices. Innovative ideas often result in simple, low cost but effective solutions. One organization that employed a receptionist who was visually impaired hung a set of wind chimes just inside the door instead of installing an expensive electronic eye that indicates when someone enters the office. Each time the door opened, the chimes rang gently, and the receptionist knew that a visitor had arrived.

Prior to purchasing high tech equipment, it is important to evaluate the specific needs of the employee and the tasks that the equipment will perform. For example, if an employee will use a braille printer only on an occasional basis, a slower printer may be a better and less costly purchase than a high speed printer. At times, low tech and high tech work together to solve practical problems. Individuals with motor impairments may find that an oversized keyboard with larger keys enables them to type with fewer errors. Extended keys on a dictating machine provide individuals with poor motor control the extra leverage needed to push "record" or "play" buttons.

Both the psychological and intellectual needs of the individual should be considered when developing a plan for assistive technology. According to Kauppi and Dzubak (1992), the likelihood of success is greater if the individual's intellectual strengths, personality characteristics, and expectations for the equipment are taken into account. They recommend involving the individual in the decision of which equipment to purchase and assessment of psychosocial factors at the job site prior to obtaining the equipment.

The installation of assistive technology should also be planned with co-workers in mind. A voice-recognition system that converts speech to typed text enables individuals with mobility impairments to enter text into a computer without using a keyboard. However, co-workers in the vicinity may find that the dictation prevents them from concentrating on their own work. Prior to installing this type of equipment in a given location, its effects on co-workers should be investigated. Once the equipment has been installed, even though it may be easily moved, the co-workers who are disturbed may be reluctant to request the change, and the person using the equipment may feel uncomfortable if such a change must be made. Individuals who use speech synthesizers should expect to use headphones to avoid disturbing co-workers.

Specially adapted equipment for individuals with disabilities may also prove useful to employees who do not have disabilities. The auditory feedback provided by speech

61

synthesizers for individuals who are visually impaired or blind may also relieve eyestrain and visual fatigue for employees without vision problems. Similarly, workstations designed for individuals with mobility impairments may diminish discomfort and fatigue for all workers. Conversely, some devices that were designed for workers without disabilities have found a market among employees who have disabilities. The mouse was designed for use with regular computers; for individuals with mobility impairments, it is a useful device for saving many keystrokes. Voice recognition systems may have been designed so that busy professionals could dictate their documents and have their speech patterns recognized by the computer system. This type of system is valuable to individuals with severe mobility impairments who are unable to use keyboards or other types of adapted equipment to enter data into a computer.

LEARNING TO USE ASSISTIVE TECHNOLOGY

After needs are assessed and recommendations for assistive technology made, how and where does the individual with a disability learn to use the equipment? On-the-job training is just one of many options. Some individuals with disabilities learn to use computers as part of their treatment at a rehabilitation hospital or in individual rehabilitation programs sponsored by state vocational rehabilitation agencies. Occupational therapists, rehabilitation engineers, or speech pathologists may provide instruction in the use of switches, mouthsticks, and head and optical pointers to operate computer keyboards. Independent living centers and community organizations that serve individuals with disabilities may provide training through center-based or home instruction. Community colleges, adult education programs, vocational-technical schools, and continuing education programs offer computer courses, although instructors may not be familiar with assistive technology. Check with the office that serves students with disabilities at these institutions to learn about special courses.

Some equipment dealers also offer training as part of the purchase agreement. Self-study courses on audiocassette and videotape are available at computer stores and bookstores. Many public libraries and universities have computer access centers, where individuals with disabilities may use specialized equipment. Libraries often have computer training manuals, audiocassettes, and videotapes in their collections.

Computer user groups are another alternative. In many cities, user groups offer technical assistance, workshops, and resource directories of members who use special computer applications and are willing to share their expertise. Members often can share information about world wide web sites that provide special information and free software programs that other users have developed (shareware).

TECHNOLOGY-RELATED ASSISTANCE FOR INDIVIDUALS WITH DISABILITIES ACT

The *Technology-Related Assistance for Individuals with Disabilities Act of 1988* (P.L. 100-407) established a program of state grants to develop comprehensive assistive technology services. One of the seven statutory purposes of the Act is to increase "the availability of and funding for the provision of assistive technology and services for individuals with disabilities" (U.S. Department of Education: 1989a).

The Act defines an *assistive technology device* as an item, piece of equipment, or system which is used to increase, maintain, or improve the functional capability of an individual with a disability. The device may be purchased commercially or modified to meet the individual's needs (U.S. Department of Education: 1989a).

An *assistive technology service* is defined as any service which helps individuals with disabilities select, acquire, or use an assistive technology device. Assistive technology services may perform functional evaluations of individuals with disabilities to determine the individual's needs for technology; enable the individual to purchase or lease assistive technology; work with the individual in the selection, adaptation, or use of assistive technology; and provide training for both individuals with disabilities and professionals, such as employers, educators, and rehabilitation professionals (U.S. Department of Education: 1989b).

The *Technology-Related Assistance for Individuals with Disabilities Act Amendments of 1994* (P.L. 103-218) strengthen the original Act. The Act mandates state-wide programs for technology-related assistance to determine needs and resources; to provide technical assistance and information; and to develop demonstration and innovation projects, training programs, and public awareness programs. The amendments set priorities for consumer responsiveness, advocacy, systems change, and outreach to underrepresented populations such as the poor, individuals in rural areas, and minorities.

SUGGESTIONS FOR PURCHASING AND INSTALLING ASSISTIVE TECHNOLOGY

Although most of the following suggestions apply to the purchase of assistive computer equipment, they should be considered when purchasing other equipment as well.

- Prior to purchasing equipment, analyze the tasks that it will perform and the functional abilities of the employee.

- Collect literature on equipment offered by a wide variety of vendors. Prices, models, and availability change rapidly, so do not rely on outdated literature. Major vendors are listed in appropriate chapters of this book, and many have toll-free numbers and web sites. Check newspapers and computer magazines for exhibits of computer equipment in your area. Some independent living centers, libraries, universities, and agencies that serve individuals with disabilities have equipment on display, or their own employees may use adapted equipment.

- Documentation and manuals should be available in an accessible format. A system that produces braille output and has a manual in print only is useless to someone who is blind.

- After collecting product literature and honing in on the products that seem most appropriate, call the vendors and ask for a demonstration in the employee's office. Be prepared to provide the company's representative with a real application of the type of work the equipment will be expected to perform. If the performance is acceptable, ask the representative for the names of other users in the local area. Phone the references and ask about the equipment's good and bad features; ease of use; reliability; the company's repair record; and compatibility with peripheral equipment. Also talk to other users who are members of user groups or independent living centers. Most people enjoy talking about their "high tech" experiences.

• The individual who will use the equipment at work should use the equipment prior to purchase to ensure that he or she is comfortable with it and that it meets the needs of the job to be performed. If possible, the employee should have a trial period in his or her own office, with the equipment hooked up to peripherals. This will ensure that the equipment is compatible with other hardware and software in the office.

• The noise level of the equipment should be evaluated to ensure that co-workers are not disturbed. Equipment such as speech synthesizers and braille printers may be quite noisy. It is wise to investigate the availability of headphones and printer hoods to reduce the noise level.

• The amount and type of technical support included with the purchase should be guaranteed in writing from the vendor. Some vendors offer unlimited toll-free support, while others offer little or no support.

• If training in the use of the equipment is necessary, be certain that accessible programs are available in the geographical area. Enrolling in a training program prior to purchasing equipment enables potential users to have a trial period while learning to use the equipment. Be certain that the course offers hands-on training with current models of the equipment.

• Purchase hardware and software that enable employees with disabilities to work jointly with colleagues. If the employee works in a graphics department that uses Macintosh computers, adapt the Macintosh. If the employee works in a department that uses PCs and everyone uses one word processing program, adapt the same system. Having compatible equipment will allow the employee to contribute to jointly written documents or graphics.

References

U.S. Department of Education

1989a   "State Grants Program for Technology-Related Assistance for Individuals with Disabilities" <u>Federal Register</u> 54:(August 9)152:32771-2

1989b   "Making the Promise of Technology a Reality" <u>OSERS News in Print</u> Office of Special Education and Rehabilitative Services 2:1

ORGANIZATIONS

For resources related to a specific disability, see the appropriate chapter, i.e., "Hearing and Speech Impairments," "Mobility Impairments," and "Visual Impairment and Blindness."

ABLEDATA
8630 Fenton Street, Suite 930
Silver Spring, MD 20910
(800) 227-0216   (301) 608-8912 (TTY)   FAX
(301) 608-8958   abledata@omcmacro.com   www.abledata.com

This database of more than 20,000 products that are currently available may be search on the web site by keyword, product type, or manufacturer. Free. Searches available in print and alternate formats. First 50 listings, $5.00; 51 to 100, $10.00. The Assistive Technology Directory lists of products. $39.00; may be downloaded from the web site, free.

Alliance for Technology Access
1304 Southpoint Boulevard, Suite 240
Petaluma, CA 94954
(707)778-3011   (707) 778-3015 (TTY)   FAX (707) 765-2080
ATAinfo@ATAccess.org   www.ATAccess.org

Operates Alliance Technology Resource Centers which provide access to assistive technology for individuals with disabilities. Services include information and resources, workshops, user groups, technical support, and hands-on demonstrations. Centers are located in many states.

Apple Computer, Inc.
Worldwide Disability Solutions
One Infinite Loop
Cupertino, CA 95014
(800) 767-2775   www.apple.com/disability/easyaccess.html

This web site describes accessibility features of Macintosh equipment as well as third party software designed for the computers. Free

Center for Assistive Technology and Environmental Accessibility (CATEA)
Georgia Institute of Technology
490 10th Street, NW
Atlanta, GA 30332-0156
(800) 726-9119   (404) 894-4960 (V/TTY)
FAX (404) 894-9320   www.catea.org

This federally funded center operates numerous projects that are devoted to the research and development, and evaluation of assistive technology and environmental accessibility.

"TechKnowledge," an information clearinghouse on assistive technology, and "Barrier Free Education," a web site that provides resources for inclusion of students with disabilities in science and math education. Assistive tech.net is a web site that has a searchable database of assistive technology products. For a complete list of projects operated by CATEA, go to the web site and click on "projects." The various web sites have their own e-mail addresses, and some have their own newsletters.

Center for Information Technology Accommodation (CITA)
General Services Administration (GSA)
1800 F Street, NW, Room 1216, MC:MKC
Washington, DC 20405
(202) 501-4906   (202) 501-2010 (TTY)
FAX (202) 501-6269   www.section508.gov

Provides federal managers with information about technology for employees with disabilities. Commonly used hardware, software, and workstations are available at a demonstration/resource center called the AT Showcase, at the GSA Central Office, Room 1216. The web site provides links to some of the items displayed at the showcase.

Computer/Electronic Accommodations Program (CAP)
5111 Leesburg Pike, Suite 810
Falls Church, VA 22041
(703) 681-8811   (703) 681-0881 (TTY)
FAX (703) 681-9075   cap@trma.osd.mil   www.tricare.osd.mil/cap

Provides computer accommodations and services to employees with disabilities who work in the Department of Defense. Participates in Workforce Recruitment Program for College Students with Disabilities. CAP is conducting a nationwide demonstration of flexiplace employment, also called telecommuting, for people with disabilities.

Disability and Business Technology Assistance Centers (DBTAC)
(800) 949-4232 (V/TTY)   www.adata.org

These regional centers, funded by the National Institute on Disability and Rehabilitation Research, provide information, training, and assistance to employers about the Americans with Disabilities Act to employers and individuals with disabilities. Calling the number above automatically links you to the center in your region.

Job Accommodation Network (JAN)
West Virginia University
PO Box 6080
Morgantown, WV 26506-6080
(800) 526-7234   (800) 232-9675 (V/TTY)   (304) 293-7186 (V/TTY)
FAX (304) 293-5407   jan@jan.wvu.edu

Maintains a database of products that facilitate accommodation in the workplace. Provides information to employers about practical accommodations which enable them to employ individuals with disabilities. Advises individuals and businesses about the Americans with Disabilities Act.

Microsoft Corporation
One Microsoft Way
Redmond, WA 98052-6393
(800) 426-9400   (800) 892-5234 (TTY)
www.microsoft.com/enable

Microsoft offers built-in accessibility in its operating system that allows individuals with disabilities to customize their computers. Accessibility features include keyboard layouts, mouse input, screen enlarger utilities, voice input utilities, and training products. Web site has guidelines for accommodations by disability and a report on the use of adapted computer technology by people with disabilities (www.microsfot.com/enable/research).

Rehabilitation Engineering and Assistive Technology Society of North America/RESNA
1700 North Moore Street, Suite 1540
Arlington, VA 22209
(703) 524-6686   (703) 524-6639 (TTY)   FAX (703) 524-6630
info@resna.org   www.resna.org

Interdisciplinary membership organization for the advancement of rehabilitation and assistive technology. Special interest groups include job accommodation, computer applications, and universal access. Professional specialty groups for manufacturers and suppliers of rehabilitation products, rehabilitation engineers, occupational therapists, and other professionals. Holds an annual conference. Membership, $150.00, includes semi-annual journal, "Assistive Technology," and quarterly "RESNA Newsletter." Subscription to "Assistive Technology" only, individuals, $65.00; institutions, $75.00.

Rehabilitation Engineering Research Center on Workplace Accommodations
Center for Assistive Technology and Environmental Accessibility (CATEA)
Georgia Institute of Technology
490 10th Street, NW
Atlanta, GA 30332-0156
(800) 726-9119   (404) 894-4960 (V/TTY)
FAX (404) 894-9320   www.catea.org/workplace.html

This federally funded project develops, designs, and promotes new assistive devices that help people with disabilities in the work environment. Also provides training on universal design.

Research and Training Center on Rural Rehabilitation
52 Corbin Hall
University of Montana
Missoula, MT 59812
(800) 732-0323 (V/TTY)   (406) 243-5467 (V/TTY)
FAX (406) 243-4730   muarid@selway.umt.edu   ruralinstitute.umt.edu

A federally funded center that conducts research and training on issues that affect service delivery of rehabilitation in rural areas. Maintains a directory of rural disability services throughout the country. Publishes a newsletter, "The Rural Exchange." Free. Available in alternate formats and on the web site.

Tech Connections
Center for Assistive Technology and Environmental Accessibility (CATEA)
Georgia Institute of Technology
490 10th Street, NW
Atlanta, GA 30332-0156
(877) 835-7335   (404) 894-4960 (V/TTY)
FAX (404) 894-9320   www.techconnections.org

The goal of Tech Connections is to increase the utilization of existing and new technologies among vocational rehabilitation counselors, people with disabilities, and employers. Provides information and training. Monthly electronic newsletter "Tech Connections" with current information on vocational rehabilitation and assistive technology. Free

Trace Research and Development Center
University of Wisconsin-Madison
2107 Engineering Center Building
1550 Engineering Drive
Madison, WI 53706
(608) 262-6966   (608) 263-5408 (TTY)
FAX (608) 262-8848   info@trace.wisc.edu   trace.wisc.edu

Conducts research to make off-the-shelf technology more accessible to individuals with disabilities through universal design.

Adaptive Technologies for Learning & Work Environments
by Joseph J. Lazzaro
Customer Service
American Library Association Order Fulfillment
PO Box 932501
Atlanta, GA 31193-2501
(866) 746-7252   (770) 280-4155   FAX (770) 2280-4155
ala-orders@pbd.com   www.alastore.ala.org

This book explores assistive technology designed for use by individuals with disabilities, including blindness and visual impairment, deafness and hearing impairment, and motor and/or speech impairments. It focuses on personal computer hardware and software and applications such as computer networks, online services, and CD-ROM. It also lists funding sources, training and technical support resources, and equipment vendors. $50.00

Assistive Devices for Use with Personal Computers
National Library Service for the Blind and Physically Handicapped (NLS)
1291 Taylor Street, NW
Washington, DC 20542
(800) 424-8567 or 8572 (Reference Section)
(800) 424-9100 (to receive application)
(202) 707-5100   (202) 707-0744 (TTY)   FAX (202) 707-0712
nls@loc.gov   www.loc.gov/nls

This reference circular describes screen readers, screen magnifiers, speech synthesizers, web browsers for people who are visually impaired, and braille interface and display devices as well as sources for these devices. Selected Internet resources are listed. Free. Also available on the web site.

Closing the Gap
PO Box 68
Henderson, MN 56044
(507) 248-3294   FAX (507) 248-3810
info@closingthegap.com   www.closingthegap.com

This bimonthly newsletter reviews hardware and software products developed for users with disabilities; $34.00. February/March issue is a resource guide of hardware and software. Resource guide may be purchased separately for $14.95. Web site has archives of articles that can be searched by keyword. The organization also provides training and consulting services and holds an annual conference.

Computer Accessibility Technology Packet
Office of Special Education and Rehabilitative Service (OSERS)
Department of Education
Room 3132 Switzer Building
Washington, DC 20202-2524
(202) 205-8241   (202) 205-4208 (TTY)
www.ed.gov/offices/OSERS/whatsnew/techpack.htm

This packet provides information about state and local education agencies' responsibilities for the technology needs of students. Includes the technical aspects of access, legal obligations concerning technology and individuals with disabilities, and a resource list. Available in print, large print, braille, audiocassette, and disk. Free/ Also available on the web site.

Computer and Web Resources for People with Disabilities
Alliance for Technology Access
1304 Southpoint Boulevard, Suite 240
Petaluma, CA 94954
(707)778-3011   (707) 778-3015 (TTY)   FAX (707) 765-2080
ATAinfo@ATAccess.org   www.ATAccess.org

This book guides readers in making decisions based on personal goals and resources related to assistive technology. Includes resource list of organizations and vendors. Softcover, $20.00; spiral bound, $27.95; HTML on CD, $27.95.

The Gate: The Guide to Assistive Technology Experience
ORCCA Technology
444 East Main Street
Lexington, KY 40507
(859) 226-9625   FAX (859) 226-0936   orcca@orccaa.com
www.orcca.com

This interactive, multimedia CD-ROM depicts individuals with disabilities using assistive technology in their everyday lives at work, home, school, and at play. Available for Windows and Macintosh. $30.00

Journal of Rehabilitation Research and Development (JRRD)
Scientific and Technical Publications Section
Rehabilitation Research and Development Service
103 South Gay Street
Baltimore, MD 21202
(410) 962-1800   FAX (410) 962-9670   pubs@vard.org
www.vard.org
A bimonthly journal that includes articles on disability, rehabilitation, sensory aids, gerontology, and disabling conditions. Available in standard print and on the web site. Free

Magazines on Audiocassette
Associated Services for the Blind
919 Walnut Street, 2nd Floor
Philadelphia, PA 19107
(215) 627-0600, extension 208   FAX (215) 922-0692
www.asb.org

Subscriptions on 4-track audiocassette for popular computer magazines such as "Computers," "Computerworld," and "Macuser" which are not available in special media elsewhere. Free price list.

National Braille Press
88 St. Stephen Street
Boston, MA 02115
(888) 965-8965   (617) 266-6160   FAX (617) 437-0456
orders@nbp.org   www.nbp.org

Publishes computer tutorials for word processing and database programs, computer braille codes in various formats, including print, audiocassette, PC disk, and braille. Free catalogue available in large print and braille. Also available on the web site.

Rural Assistive Technology Slide Presentation Resource
Breaking New Ground Resource Center
Purdue University
1146 Agricultural Engineering Building
West Lafayette, IN 47907-1146
(800) 825-4264   (765) 494-5088 (V/TTY)   FAX (765)96-1356
www.breakingnewground.info

Both low and high tech solutions for farmers and ranchers with disabilities are depicted in this set of 134 slides. $100.00

Voice Recognition Technology
PACER Center (Parent Advocacy Coalition for Educational Rights)
8161 Normandale Boulevard
Minneapolis, MN 55437
(888) 248-0822   (952) 838-9000
In MN, (800) 537-2237   (952) 838-0190 (TTY)
FAX (952) 838-0199   pacer@pacer.org   www.pacer.org

This publication discusses how voice recognition can help people with disabilities. It discusses the latest technology and provides a list of vendors and web sites. $3.00

FINANCING ASSISTIVE TECHNOLOGY

Many individuals with disabilities who require assistive technology do not have the financial resources to purchase it. Implementation of the Americans with Disabilities Act improves the situation for many job applicants and employees. In addition, a variety of funding sources are available, including vocational rehabilitation agencies, third party payers such as disability insurance, foundations, and community service organizations.

Medical resources which may be tapped for funding assistive technology include insurance companies, which may require a "claim of medical necessity," signed by a physician. Many insurance companies view assistive technology as a cost effective means to return an individual to work. Medicare pays the cost of durable medical equipment (DME) which serves a medical purpose and is used in the home. Some equipment, such as a wheelchair, may be required both in the home and in the workplace. Medicare's Six-Point Plan spells out reimbursement procedures for various equipment categories. Medicaid's optional services may cover prosthetic equipment and rehabilitative services.

Vocational services provided through state rehabilitation agencies include a comprehensive evaluation with recommendations for assistive technology which will enable the individual to return to work. The Individualized Written Rehabilitation Program (IWRP) may require that the state vocational rehabilitation agency purchase assistive technology and provide training in use of the equipment. Some states provide full funding; others provide partial funding. Employers may also pay for assistive technology through a cost-sharing plan in conjunction with the state agency.

The Social Security Administration offers several incentive programs to encourage individuals to return to work. The Plan for Achieving Self-Support (PASS) allows individuals with disabilities who are receiving Supplemental Security Income (SSI) to set aside the income to obtain funding for assistive technology. The Social Security Administration will provide information about this program upon request, (800) 772-1213 or (800) 325-0778 (TTY).

Individuals who are receiving Social Security Disability Insurance (SSDI) benefits may be granted a Trial Work Period, which provides an opportunity to return to work without loss of benefits. Individuals may work for up to nine months in a five year period during which time earnings are more than the substantial gainful activity level ($700 per month as of July 1, 1999; $1100, for legally blind recipients) without affecting benefits. Months in which earnings do not exceed the substantial gainful activity level are not counted toward the trial work period. After completion of nine months with substantial gainful activity, individuals may receive benefits during a three year extended period for any month in which their earnings are not at the substantial gainful activity level. The cost of purchasing assistive technology is deducted from the gross income; if net income is within the limits for substantial gainful activity, benefits will continue.

Individuals who receive either SSI or SSDI benefits may have the cost of disability-related equipment or services which are required for their work deducted from income to determine substantial gainful activity. Impairment-Related Work Expenses (IRWE) must be paid for by the individual, not reimbursed by a third party. Deductibility depends on how and when the equipment is used. IRWE expenses may include items such as wheelchairs, text telephones, expenses incurred in using service dogs (guide dogs for individuals who are visually impaired or blind or hearing dogs for individuals who are deaf or hearing impaired), or modified vehicles for traveling to and from work.

Several equipment vendors offer special programs which enable individuals to acquire equipment at discounted prices. Ask if such a program is available prior to purchasing.

Community-based service organizations such as the Lions Clubs, Rotary, Quota, and others may provide assistance to individuals for the purchase of assistive technology. Local Chambers of Commerce can refer individuals to these organizations.

References

Kauppi, Dwight R. and Cora M. Dzubak
1992   "Psychosocial Factors in Assistive Technology and Employment" Technology and Disability 1(4):23-28

Directory of Computer and High Technology Grants
and
Directory of Grants for Organizations Serving People with Disabilities
Research Grant Guides
12798 West Forest Hill Boulevard, Suite 304
West Palm Beach, FL 33414
(561) 795-6129   FAX (561) 795-7794   www.researchgrant.com

These two directories provide information about funding sources nationwide. $69.00 each

Financial Aid for Students with Disabilities
HEATH Resource Center
George Washington University
2121 K Street, NW, Suite 220
Washington, DC 20037
(800) 544-3284 (V/TTY)   (202) 973-0904 (V/TTY)
FAX (202) 973-0908   askheath@heath.gwu.edu   www.heath.gwu.edu

This publication covers grants, loans, work-study programs, vocational rehabilitation services, and organizations that provide scholarships. Free. Also available on the web site.

Financial Aid for the Disabled and Their Families
by Gail Ann Schlachter and R. David Weber
Reference Service Press
5000 Windplay Drive, Suite 4
El Dorado Hills, CA 95762
(916) 939-9620   FAX (916) 939-9626
www.rspfunding.com

A directory of scholarships, fellowships, loans, and awards for individuals with disabilities. $40.00

Study on the Financing of Assistive Technology Devices and Services for Individuals with Disabilities
National Council on Disability (NCD)
1331 F Street, NW, Suite 1050
Washington, DC 20004-1107
(202) 272-2004   (202) 272-2074 (TTY)   FAX (202) 272-2022
mquigley@ncd.gov   www.ncd.gov

A congressionally mandated study, this report analyzes federal laws and policies; health insurers' coverage of the costs of assistive technology; alternative funding sources; and lending practices of financial institutions. The perspectives of individuals who use assistive technology are also presented. Free. Also available on the web site.

Chapter 5

TRANSITION FROM SCHOOL TO WORK

Young people with severe disabilities often require extra services, counseling, and training to make the transition from the school setting to a work setting. Provided with the training, equipment, and counseling that they need, many individuals with severe disabilities are able to enter the competitive job market. The type of placements that individuals with severe disabilities obtain will vary. Some individuals with severe physical disabilities but no cognitive disabilities may obtain positions in the competitive job market; others may need on-going support (see "SUPPORTED EMPLOYMENT" section below); and still others may find employment in sheltered workshops. The ability of young people with severe disabilities to obtain employment is, of course, in large part dependent upon the attitudes of employers, supervisors, and co-workers.

The *School-to-Work Opportunities Act* (P.L. 103-239) passed in 1994 set federal policies for school-to-work transition for all youths, including those with disabilities. The student's successful transition from school to work requires the cooperation of special educators, vocational rehabilitation professionals, parents, and employers. Many state vocational rehabilitation agencies have assigned a staff person to act as a liaison with school systems (DeCaro et al.: 1990). All agencies involved should enter agreements that spell out their specific roles. In many instances, employers enter into cooperative agreements with schools to provide training to the students (Berkell and Gaylord-Ross: 1989).

It is in the student's best interest to develop a plan with realistic goals for employment. The *Individuals with Disabilities Education Act* (IDEA, P.L. 101-476; reauthorized in 1997 as P.L. 105-17) requires that transition services and plans be included in the student's individualized education plan (IEP) by the time he or she reaches age 16. The individualized transition plan (ITP) should be continuously updated, based on an analysis of the student's abilities and environment and should take account of the student's living conditions (Schalock: 1986). Some students may begin their work experience part-time while still attending school.

Regulations put forth following the passage of the 1997 IDEA are available at several web sites, including the U.S. Department of Education and Wright's Law (see "ORGANIZATIONS" section below).

Section 504 of the Rehabilitation Act prohibits programs that receive federal financial assistance from discriminating against individuals with disabilities who are otherwise eligible to benefit from their programs. Virtually all educational institutions are affected by this law, including private postsecondary institutions which receive federal financial assistance under a wide variety of programs. In order to comply with the law, most postsecondary institutions have established offices to provide services to students with disabilities. Programs must be physically accessible to individuals with disabilities, and construction must be designed so that it is in compliance with standard specifications for accessibility. In addition to counseling services, tests in special media, special assistive technology, and accessible physical facilities for classrooms must be provided.

Despite the federal initiatives to increase opportunities for students, a study found that students with disabilities enroll in postsecondary institutions at only one-quarter the rate of students without disabilities (Fairweather and Shaver: 1991). The discrepancy in attendance rates between students with disabilities and those without disabilities is greater for four year colleges than for community colleges. However, students with disabilities are as likely to attend postsecondary vocational schools as their cohorts who are not disabled. Students with sensory impairments have the highest attendance rates at postsecondary institutions, and students with orthopedic, emotional, or learning disabilities have the lowest rates.

SUPPORTED EMPLOYMENT

Supported employment is paid employment with support provided at the workplace for people with severe disabilities who otherwise would not be able to obtain competitive employment. The goal of supported employment is to provide employment opportunities to people who are unemployed or who live in residential facilities and would be able to return to the community if they were employed. Supported employment is appropriate for individuals with mental retardation, emotional illness, or severe physical disabilities, although it has been used most frequently for people with mental retardation and mental illness (Wehman et al.: 1990; West et al.: 1992). Supported employment provides training for obtaining a job; help with transportation in getting to the workplace; and training and ongoing support at the workplace.

Traditionally, supervision and assistance at the work site have been provided by a job coach, who accompanies the individual to work on the first day of employment and continues to observe the employee for a while; then he or she begins to observe the employee less frequently and ultimately stops. Controversy about the role of the job coach has developed. Some observers have suggested that "natural" or "internal" supports be provided by supervisors, co-workers, and traditional business resources at the place of employment, eliminating the stigma of a job coach (Fabian and Luecking: 1991; Rhodes et al.: 1991). This alternative approach is more likely to achieve maximum integration of the employee in the workplace.

Individuals who need special training to obtain supported employment may use funds they receive from the PASS program of the Social Security Administration to pay for this training (see Chapter 2, "Federal Laws and Programs"). At the same time, they may continue to receive SSI benefits.

The concept of supported employment has been sanctioned through a number of federal laws. Supported employment, as defined by the 1986 amendments to the Rehabilitation Act, requires that employment take place in a competitive setting and that workers with disabilities be integrated with workers who are not disabled. The Rehabilitation Services Administration is authorized to provide grants to state, public, and private organizations to develop programs of supported employment.

There are several different models of supported employment (Abberbock: 1991; Sowers and Power: 1991). The use of "enclaves" involves employing up to eight individuals who work together as a team under close supervision. "Mobile crews" travel together to different businesses, usually as custodians or grounds keepers. In the "small business model," up to eight individuals work together as a business to produce one product or service. This model has been criticized because it is unlikely to achieve the goal of integration with workers who are not disabled. In the "individual placement model," a job coach assesses, trains, places, and observes an individual at the workplace. As noted above, some observers have suggested that the individual placement model utilize "natural" or "internal" supports instead of a job coach.

Federal initiatives have undoubtedly increased the employment rates for students with severe disabilities. Nonetheless, young people with disabilities are far less likely to be employed than their cohorts who are not disabled. Outreach programs to educate employers and supervisors about the capabilities of people with severe disabilities and to encourage potential employers to participate in transition programs and supported employment programs are important steps in increasing employment opportunities.

References

Abberbock, Ellen
1991   "Supported Employment" Independent Living May/June 63-64
Berkell, Dianne E. and Robert Gaylord-Ross
1989   "The Concept of Transition: Historical and Current Developments" pp. 1-21 in Dianne E. Berkell and James M. Brown (eds.) Transition from School to Work New York, NY: Longman
DeCaro, James et al.
1990   "A Partnership between Rehabilitation and Postsecondary Education" pp. 37-53 in Douglas Watson (ed.) Model State Plan for Rehabilitation of Individuals Who are Deaf and Hard-of-Hearing Little Rock, AR: Arkansas Rehabilitation Research and Training Center on Deafness and Hearing Impairment
Fabian, Ellen S. and Richard G. Luecking
1991   "Doing it the Company Way: Using Internal Company Supports in the Workplace" Journal of Applied Rehabilitation Counseling 22(2):32-35
Fairweather, James S. and Debra M. Shaver
1991   "Making the Transition to Postsecondary Education and Training" Exceptional Children December/January 264-270
Rhodes, Larry, Dennis Sandow, David Mank, Jay Buckley, and Joyce Albin
1991   "Expanding the Role of Employers in Supported Employment" JASH 16(4):213-217
Schalock, Robert L.
1986   "Service Delivery Coordination" pp. 115-127 in Frank R. Rusch (ed.) Competitive Employment Issues and Strategies Baltimore, MD: Brookes Publishing
Sowers, Jo-Ann and Laurie Powers
1991   Vocational Preparation and Employment of Students with Physical and Multiple Disabilities Baltimore, MD: Brookes Publishing Co.

Wehman Paul, et al.

1990   "The National Supported Employment Initiative" <u>OSERS News in Print</u> III:(Winter):3:7-13

West, Michael, W. Grant Revell, and Paul Wehman

1992   "Achievement and Challenges I: A Five-Year Report on Consumer and System Outcomes from the Supported Employment Initiative" <u>JASH</u> 28(24):227-235

Association for Career and Technical Education (ACTE)
1410 King Street
Alexandria, VA 22314
(800) 826-9972   (703) 683-3111   FAX (703) 683-7424
acte@acteonline.org   www.acteonline.org

Professional association for individuals who work in the field of vocational education. Many special divisions including a Special Needs Division and a Technology Education Division. Membership, $60.00, includes newsletter, "Techniques."

Association for Persons in Supported Employment (APSE)
1627 Monument Avenue
Richmond, VA 23220
(804) 278-9187   FAX (804) 278-9377   www.apse.org

A membership organization for service providers, consumers, and employers, APSE advocates for increased and improved opportunities for supported employment for individuals with severe disabilities. Holds annual conference. Membership fee for individuals depends upon income level; organizations, $640.00. Membership includes quarterly newsletter, "Advance," and "Journal of Vocational Rehabilitation" online.

Association on Higher Education and Disability (AHEAD)
PO Box 54066
Waltham, MA 02454
(781) 788-0003 (V/TTY)   FAX (781) 788-0033
ahead@ahead.org   www.ahead.org

Promotes the full participation of individuals with disabilities in postsecondary education. Special interest groups focus on specific disabilities, technology, and other topics. Membership, professionals, $150.00, includes bimonthly newsletter, "Alert," and quarterly "Journal of Postsecondary Education and Disability;" other categories include affiliate, institutional, and student memberships.

Bridges. . . from School to Work
Marriott Foundation for People with Disabilities
One Marriott Drive
Washington, DC 20058
(301) 380-7771   (301) 380-6680 (TTY)   FAX (301) 380-8973
www.marriottfoundation.org

Develops internship programs in businesses for students in their final year of high school. Programs are administered by agencies in local communities. Students are recommended by school systems, which maintain contacts with employers. Also provides training to employees in cooperating businesses.

Cornell University Program on Employment and Disability
New York State School of Industrial and Labor Relations, Extension Division
106 ILR Extension Building
Ithaca, NY 14853
(607) 255-7797   (607) 255-2891 (TTY)   FAX (607) 255-2763
ilru_ped@cornell.edu   www.ilr.cornell.edu/ped

This program seeks to improve employment practices covered by Title I of the Americans with Disabilities Act. Produces and disseminates publications on Title I, transition from school to work, and supported employment. Catalogue available on the web site. Conducts research, provides technical assistance, and conducts training programs for employers throughout the U.S. and abroad.

Council for Exceptional Children (CEC)
1110 North Glebe Road, Suite 300
Arlington, VA 22201
(888) 232-7733   (703) 620-3660   (703) 264-9446 (TTY)
FAX (703) 264-9494   service@cec.sped.org   www.cec.sped.org

A professional membership organization that works toward improving the quality of education for children who have disabilities or are gifted. Membership fees vary by geographical location. Holds annual conference. Has special Division of Career Development and Transition. Publishes journals "Teaching Exceptional Children," ($63.00) and "Exceptional Children Today" ($63.00). Membership includes these two journals plus newsletter, "Exceptional Children," published quarterly,

ERIC (Educational Resources Information Center)
(800) 538-3742   www.eric.gov

Funded by the U.S. Department of Education, this database includes bibliographic references and full texts of articles and monographs. Includes information on transition from school to work and disability.

National Clearinghouse on Postsecondary Education for Individuals with Disabilities
HEATH Resource Center
George Washington University
2121 K Street, NW, Suite 220
Washington, DC 20037
(800) 544-3284 (V/TTY)   (202) 973-0904 (V/TTY)
FAX (202) 973-0908   askheath@heath.gwu.edu   www.heath.gwu.edu

A clearinghouse that provides information about postsecondary education. Answers telephone inquiries and produces a variety of publications related to postsecondary education for students with disabilities and preparation for employment. Newsletter, "Information from HEATH," available on web site only. Archives also available on the web site.

National Dissemination Center for Children with Disabilities
[formerly National Information Center For Children and Youth with Disabilities (NICHCY)]
PO Box 1492
Washington, DC 20013
(800) 695-0285 (V/TTY)   FAX (202) 884-8441
nichcy@aed.org   www.nichcy.org

Provides information and referral, technical assistance, and publications to parents, educators, caregivers, and advocates. Special focus on "IDEA" and "No Child Left Behind" laws. Newsletter, "News Digest." Free. Publications are in English and Spanish and are available on the web site.

National Resource Center on Supported Living and Choice
Center on Human Policy
Syracuse University
805 South Crouse Avenue
Syracuse, NY 13244-2280
(800) 894-0826   (315) 443-3851   (315) 443-4355 (TTY)
FAX (315) 443-4338   thechp@aued.syr.edu
hsoeweb.syr.edu/thechp

A federally funded center that conducts research and advocates to ensure the rights and full inclusion of people with developmental disabilities in community life. Produces a variety of publications and slide shows, including those related to supported employment.

Office of Special Education Programs (OSEP)
U.S. Department of Education
400 Maryland Avenue, SW
Switzer Building, Room 3086
Washington, DC 20202
(202) 205-5507   (202) 205-8170 (TTY)   FAX (202) 205-9070
www.ed.gov/about/offices/list/om/fs_po/osers/special.html

Provides grants to state vocational rehabilitation and education agencies for special programs for transition from school to work.

PACER Center (Parent Advocacy Coalition for Educational Rights)
8161 Normandale Boulevard
Minneapolis, MN 55437
(888) 248-0822   (952) 838-9000
In MN, (800) 537-2237   (952) 838-0190 (TTY)
FAX (952) 838-0199   pacer@pacer.org   www.pacer.org

A coalition of disability organizations that offers information about laws, procedures, and parents' rights and responsibilities. Publishes "PACESETTER," three times a year, free, and "Early Childhood Connection," for parents of young children with disabilities, three times a year, free. Also publishes "The Computer Monitor," a newsletter that deals with assistive technology for students with disabilities, free. Free catalogue of publications available. Free

Projects with Industry (PWI)
Office of Special Education and Rehabilitation Services OSERS
U.S. Department of Education
400 Maryland Avenue, SW, Room 3332
Washington, DC 20202-2740
(202) 205-8922   FAX (202) 260-9424   lavanna.weems@ed.gov
www.ed.gov/programs/rsapwi/index.html

A federally funded program authorized under the Rehabilitation Act, PWI funds programs that expand job opportunities for individuals with disabilities. Services include training, support, job development, and job placement. One priority within this program is the transition from school to work for students with disabilities.

Rehabilitation Research and Training Center on Workplace Supports
Virginia Commonwealth University
PO Box 842011
Richmond, VA 23284-2011
(804) 828-1851   (804) 828-2494 (TTY)   FAX (804) 828-2193
tcblancke@vcu.edu   www.worksupport.com

A federally funded center that conducts research on vocational programs and school to work transition. Houses the National Clearinghouse on Supported Employment. Publishes quarterly newsletter, free. Also available on the web site.

Rehabilitation Services Administration (RSA)
U.S. Department of Education
400 Maryland Avenue, SW, Room 3329-MES
Washington, DC 20202-2251
(202) 205-5482   FAX (202) 205-9874
www.ed.gov/about/offices/list/osers/osers/about.html)

The principal federal agency mandated to carry out the provisions of the Rehabilitation Act of 1973 and its amendments, RSA provides grants to state vocational rehabilitation agencies to fund programs of supported employment.

TASH: The Association for Persons with Severe Handicaps
29 West Susquehanna Avenue, Suite 210
Baltimore, MD 21204
(410) 828-8274   (410) 828-1306 (TTY)   FAX (410) 828-6706
info@tash.org   www.tash.org

Works to improve the education and increase the independence of individuals with severe disabilities. Holds annual conference. Quarterly "Research Practice for Persons with Severe Disabilities" and monthly "TASH Newsletter" (both included with membership). Regular membership, $103.00; low income, $60.00.

Transition Research Institute (TRI)
University of IL-Urbana-Champaign
113 Children's Research Center
51 Gerty Drive
Champaign, IL 61820
(217) 333-2325 (V/TTY)   FAX (217) 244-0851   nta@aed.org
www.dssc.org/uta0

This research institute identifies effective practices, provides technical assistance, and performs research to evaluate interventions related to transitions of students with disabilities. Maintains a listserv, "Tri-Talk."

Wright's Law
c/o The Special Ed Advocate
PO Box 1008
Deltaville, VA 23043
(804) 257-0857   FAX (804) 776-7605
wright@wrightslaw.com   www.wrightslaw.com

This web site provides information to help parents advocate for children with special needs. Provides updated information on federal laws that affect special education. The regulations for IDEA the status of the law's reauthorization may be found on the site. Offers advocacy and law libraries. Publishes "Special Ed Advocate" newsletter; available on web site only.

Access Transition
by Tom Morales et al.
Alliance for Technology Access
1304 Southpoint Boulevard, Suite 240
Petaluma, CA 94954
(707)778-3011   (707) 778-3015 (TTY)
FAX (707) 765-2080   ATAinfo@ATAccess.org   www.ATAccess.org

Written for teenagers with special needs, this publication discusses the concept of transition from school to work, the need for planning, the teens' responsibilities, the role of assistive technology, and success stories. Free. Available on the web site.

Begin the Between: Planning for the Transition from High School to Adult Life
PACER Center (Parent Advocacy Coalition for Educational Rights)
8161 Normandale Boulevard
Minneapolis, MN 55437
(888) 248-0822   (952) 838-9000
In MN, (800) 537-2237   (952) 838-0190 (TTY)
FAX (952) 838-0199   pacer@pacer.org   www.pacer.org

A workbook that guides students and their families through the process of developing a transition plan based on the student's skills and goals. $5.00

Career Planning and Employment Strategies for Postsecondary Students
HEATH Resource Center
George Washington University
2121 K Street, NW, Suite 220
Washington, DC 20037
(800) 544-3284 (V/TTY)   (202) 973-0904 (V/TTY)
FAX (202) 973-0908   askheath@heath.gwu.edu   www.heath.gwu.edu

This guide discusses establishing and executing a plan to achieve employment goals. Includes information on campus employment counselors and resources for organizations and publications. Free. Also available on the web site.

Coaching Winners: Job Coaching for Supported Employment Programs
Program Development Associates
PO Box 2038
Syracuse, NY 13220-2038
(800) 543-2119   FAX (315) 452-0710   www.pdassoc.com

This videotape shows how job coaches perform skills assessments, develop community based sites, match potential employees with jobs, and supervise them on the job. 20 minutes. $49.00

The Complete IEP Guide
by Lawrence Siegel
Nolo Press
950 Parker Street
Berkeley, CA 94710
(800) 955-4775   FAX (800) 645-0895   order@nolo.com
www.nolo.com

Written for parents of children who are in special education, this book provides detailed information about the Individualized Education Program (IEP) and how to use legal options to resolve disputes with the educational system. $29.99

Ensuring Access, Equity and Quality for Students with Disabilities in School-to-Work Systems: A Guide to Federal Law and Policies
Institute on Community Integration
University of Minnesota
102 Pattee Hall
150 Pillsbury Drive, SE
Minneapolis, MN 55455
(612) 624-44512   FAX (612) 624-9344
publications@ici.mail.education.umn.edu
www.ici.umn.edu/ici

This guide discusses the federal legislation and policies that ensure the participation of youths with disabilities in school to work opportunities. $10.00

Everybody's Working
Program Development Associates
PO Box 2038
Syracuse, NY 13220-2038
(800) 543-2119   FAX (315) 452-0710   www.pdassoc.com

This videotape shows five young people with disabilities who are successfully employed in a variety of occupations. 22 minutes $39.00

Life Beyond the Classroom
by Paul Wehman (ed.)
Brookes Publishing Company
PO Box 10624
Baltimore, MD 21285-9945
(800) 638-3775   FAX (410) 337-8539
custserv@pbrookes.com   www.brookespublishing.com

This book provides model systems of transition, including job development and placement as well as case studies. $64.95

Meeting the Needs of Youth with Disabilities: Handbook on Supplemental Security Income Work Incentives and Transition Students
Institute on Community Integration
University of Minnesota
102 Pattee Hall
150 Pillsbury Drive, SE
Minneapolis, MN 55455
(612) 624-44512   FAX (612) 624-9344
publications@ici.mail.education.umn.edu
www.ici.umn.edu/ici

This handbook describes how Supplemental Security Income (SSI) work incentives such as Earned Income Exclusion, Impairment-Related Work Expense (IRWE), and Plan for Achieving Self-support (PASS) may be used in the IEP/transition plan for students with disabilities. $8.00.

More Than a Job: Securing Satisfying Careers for People with Disabilities
by Paul Wehman and John Kregel (eds.)
Brookes Publishing Company
PO Box 10624
Baltimore, MD 21285-9945
(800) 638-3775   FAX (410) 337-8539
custserv@pbrookes.com   www.brookespublishing.com

This book presents a consumer perspective on disability and employment. Covers employment strategies such as supported employment, vocational training, and assistive technology. $34.95

Reach for the Dream: Developing Individual Service Plans for Persons with Disabilities
TRN Training Resource Network
PO Box 439
St. Augustine, FL 32085-0439
(866) 823-9800   FAX (904) 823-3554
customerservice@trninc.com   www.trninc.com

A manual that provides suggestions for developing Individual Written Rehabilitation Programs and Individualized Education Plans with sample profiles. $20.00

Self-Directed Employment: A Handbook for Transition Teachers and Employment Specialists
by James E. Martin et al.
Brookes Publishing Company
PO Box 10624
Baltimore, MD 21285-9945
(800) 638-3775   FAX (410) 337-8539
custserv@pbrookes.com   www.brookespublishing.com

In this book, the authors present their model for fulfilling the requirements of federal laws that individuals participate in their own plan for vocational assessment, finding a job, and evaluating it. Includes case studies of individuals who have used this model and forms to provide guidance through the process. $54.95

Skills for Success: A Career Education Handbook for Children and Adolescents with Visual Impairments
by Karen E. Wolffe
AFB Press
PO Box 1020
Sewickley, PA 15143-1020
(800) 232-3044   (412) 741-1398
FAX (412) 741-0609   afbpress@afb.org   www.afb.org

This guide offers suggestions that will enable children with visual impairments to develop life skills that will lead to successful careers. $45.95

Supported Employment InfoLines
TRN Training Resource Network
PO Box 439
St. Augustine, FL 32085-0439
(866) 823-9800   FAX (904) 823-3554
customerservice@trninc.com   www.trninc.com

A newsletter with information about job development, career assessment, strategies for job coaches, co-worker relations, and transition plans. 10 issues a year. Print edition, $109.00; e-mail version, $99.00.

The Transition Handbook
by Carolyn Hughes
Brookes Publishing Company
PO Box 10624
Baltimore, MD 21285-9945
(800) 638-3775   FAX (410) 337-8539
custserv@pbrookes.com   www.brookespublishing.com

This book discusses models for transition that have been tested by research. Provides information on how to tailor these programs to the needs of individual students. $48.00

Transition Planning: A Team Effort
National Dissemination Center for Children with Disabilities (NICHCY)
PO Box 1492
Washington, DC 20013
(800) 695-0285 (V/TTY)   FAX (202) 884-8441
nichcy@aed.org   www.nichcy.org

This article provides ideas for parents, school personnel, and other providers to work together. Free. Also available on the web site.

Transition Tote System: Navigating the Rapids of Life
Navigating the Rapids of Life, videotape and booklet
American Printing House for the Blind
PO Box 6085
Louisville, KY 40206-0085
(800) 223-1839   (502) 895-2405   FAX (502) 899-2274
info@aph.org   www.aph.org

This system provides a Student Kit, which includes a manual, tote case, clipboard, calendar, and PC disk, is designed to enable students who are blind or visually impaired to prepare for the working world. The manual covers topics such as self-awareness, work exploration, job seeking skills, and job keeping skills. Available in large print, braille, or audiocassette. $75.00. Information supplements for teachers are available separately in braille, $64.00 or print, $39.00. Videotape and booklet emphasize skills needed in transition from school to work. Videotape is closed captioned and video described. $25.00

Transition to Work Inventory
Jist Publishing
8902 Otis Avenue
Indianapolis, IN 46216
(800) 648-5478   (317) 613-4200
FAX (317) 613-4309   info@jist.com   www.jist.com

This inventory, which is useful for a wide range of individuals including those who have had little or no work experience, assesses likes and dislikes and includes a career exploration chart. Package of 25, $34.95

Understanding Community Based Employment and Follow-Up Services
by K. Botterbusch
Research and Training Center
Stout Vocational Rehabilitation Institute
University of Wisconsin-Stout
PO Box 790
Menomonie, WI 54751
(715) 232-1389   (715) 232-5025   FAX (715) 232-2251
rtc@uwstout.edu   www.rtc.uwstout.edu

This publication provides information about assessment, follow-up, and models for competitive employment. Describes examples of community based employment programs in four locations. $15.00

Vocational Training News
Aspen Publications
PO Box 911
Frederick, MD 21705
(800) 655-5597   FAX (800) 561-4845
www.aspenpublishers.com

This weekly newsletter reports on school to work transition, job training, and vocational education. Available in e-mail or print versions. One year, $398.00; two years, $677.00.

Working with Pride: A Video about the Rehabilitation Act
PACER Center (Parent Advocacy Coalition for Educational Rights)
8161 Normandale Boulevard
Minneapolis, MN 55437
(888) 248-0822   (952) 838-9000
In MN, (800) 537-2237   (952) 838-0190 (TTY)
FAX (952) 838-0199   pacer@pacer.org   www.pacer.org

This videotape depicts the experiences of a high school student in transition to adult vocational rehabilitation and an adult with a disability seeking employment. 17 minutes. Open captioned. A version with audio description is also available. $35.00

Chapter 6

OLDER WORKERS

It is more difficult for older workers to obtain employment than it is for younger workers, in large part because of the ageism that exists in all aspects of society. Those who make hiring decisions often believe that older workers are less productive and more likely to be away from the office because of ill health, although several studies have found no empirical support for these negative stereotypes. Older workers with disabilities have an even more difficult time obtaining employment.

A report from the U.S. Bureau of the Census (1989) provided empirical evidence that work disability is strongly correlated with age. While only 5.6% of individuals age 25 to 34 had a work disability in 1988, four times as many individuals age 55 to 64 (22.3%) had a work disability. This finding is not surprising, in light of the general correlation between disability and aging. Sensory impairments in particular occur with great frequency in the older population. Despite the higher prevalence of disability among elders, this group receives a disproportionately small part of the rehabilitation services provided by state agencies (Holland and Falvo: 1990). Failure to provide rehabilitation services to elders reflects ageism on the part of professionals and elders' acceptance that nothing can be done to help them.

Elders with disabilities may have lived with a disability from birth, or they may have acquired a disability in mid-life or later life. Adjustment to a disability is different for those who have acquired the disability early on than for those who acquired a disability at a later stage in life. Baumann and associates (1986) note that it is important for elders to avoid fixation on the disability that in turn results in rejection of rehabilitation. They suggest that re-employment counseling and job placement can help to overcome fixation and long-term disability.

Despite the observation that age discrimination exists in the workplace, federal law specifically prohibits this type of discrimination. The *Age Discrimination in Employment Act* (P.L.90-202) (ADEA), passed by Congress in 1967, protects individuals age 40 or over from discrimination in employment, including hiring, discharge, pay, and promotions. Subsequent amendments to the ADEA have eliminated forced retirement for most workers and required equal benefits and pensions for older workers. The law applies to employers who have 20 or more employees; employment agencies; labor organizations with 25 or more members; and local, state, and federal governments. Complaints may be filed with the Equal Employment Opportunity Commission (see "ORGANIZATIONS" section below) within 180 days of the alleged discrimination.

Title V of the Older Americans Act Amendments (P.L. 106-501) mandates that the U.S. Department of Labor Employment Training Administration (ETA) fund the Senior Community Service Employment Program (SCSEP). SCSEP promotes the part-time, subsidized and unsubsidized employment of individuals who are 55 or over, whose annual income is not more than 25% over the poverty level, and who have poor prospects of employment. The Projects with Industry program, also sponsored by the federal government, provides another source of training and job placement for older workers with disabilities. In addition to federal programs, state departments on aging, state departments of labor, and community organizations often have special initiatives and programs to help older workers find employment. Employers should contact these agencies to find out how to recruit older workers; candidates for employment should obtain information about the placement services provided.

Many elders with disabilities who are employed may retain their positions by using assistive technology. Alternative computer keyboards, for example, reduce repetitive strain injuries experienced when using a standard keyboard. Elders with vision loss may find that low vision aids such as magnifiers and specially adapted computers will enable them to read and carry out other tasks. Elders with hearing loss may perform their work by using TTYs and assistive listening systems. Many of the environmental adaptations that facilitate everyday living in the home are also applicable to the workplace. Good lighting and contrast, uncluttered halls and aisles, nonskid floors, and good acoustics are examples of some of the environmental changes that will help.

Depending upon the disability and the requirements of the job, elders with disabilities may be able to remain in their current position, or they may find that it is necessary to be retrained for a new position. Services to help elders determine their best options are available from a number of sources. State rehabilitation agencies, which previously limited vocational rehabilitation to individuals age 18 to 64, now do not have age restrictions on their services (Holland and Falvo: 1990). They provide job training, job evaluation, environmental adaptations, assistive technology, and job placement.

References

Baumann, Neal J., James C. Anderson, and Malcom H. Morrison
1986   "Employment of the Older Disabled Person: Current Environment, Outlook, and Research Needs" pp. 329-342 in Stanley J. Brody and George E. Ruff (eds.) Aging and Rehabilitation New York, NY: Springer Publishing Company
Holland, Beverly E. and Donna R. Falvo
1990   "Forgotten: Elderly Persons with Disability -- A Consequence of Policy" Journal of Rehabilitation April/May/June pp. 32-35
U.S. Bureau of the Census
1989   Labor Force Status and Other Characteristics of Persons with a Work Disability: 1981 to 1988 Current Population Reports, Series P-23, No. 160 Washington, DC: U.S. Government Printing Office

Case Vignette

Elaine Williams, An Older Worker with Carpal Tunnel Syndrome

Elaine Williams is a 65 year old woman who has worked for ten years for a small company that manufactures vinyl window shades. She inserts the rolled shades into plastic bags, fastens and labels the bags, and packs them into boxes for shipping.

For several months, Elaine has been awakened at night with numbness and tingling in her hands. Recently she has also experienced pain when reaching for bags of shades to pack, occasionally dropping them. After reporting this problem to her supervisor, Elaine arranged for a medical examination, where she was diagnosed with carpal tunnel syndrome (CTS). Carpal tunnel syndrome occurs when the hand's median nerve and flexor tendons, which pass through the carpal (or wrist) tunnel, are compressed. The repetitive hand movements she has used in her work over the years have pressed the nerve against the tunnel, producing pain, tingling, and numbness.

The physician who examined Elaine recommended that she wear splints while working and sleeping, in order to relieve the pressure on her wrists. The physician referred her to a physical therapist who supplied the splints and demonstrated to Elaine how to place them on her wrists. Although Elaine has had no problem wearing these splints while she sleeps, she has found them awkward to use at work. Her production rate has declined, and she fears that she will lose her job.

Ken Short, her supervisor, has set up a meeting with Elaine and Amanda Harris, the personnel manager. Ken is concerned about Elaine's health but also needs her in the packing room so that the department can achieve its required volume of work. Amanda suggests that they consider modifying the job and investigate other positions in the company. Based on the physician's report of Elaine's condition, the company provides her with three weeks off from work to rest her hands and allow the inflammation and swelling to subside.

Prior to Elaine's return to work, she meets again with Ken and Amanda. Amanda reports that the company's office assistant has asked to reduce

Continued on next page

her hours in order to care for her elderly mother. Amanda proposes that Elaine's job be modified so that she may work part-time in the office. Over the years, Ken has relied on Elaine to orient and supervise new employees as well as meet her production rate; the proposed job sharing plan would allow Elaine to continue in this role. In addition, the company has agreed to pay for the services of an occupational therapist to assess Elaine's needs for assistive devices and environmental adaptations in both roles. Elaine is apprehensive about learning the office assistant's job but glad to have an opportunity to continue working.

Several assistive devices are provided to help Elaine perform the office assistant's duties. Although minimal typing is required, Elaine uses a computer to record messages, take orders, and occasionally type Amanda's correspondence. A wrist rest, placed under the computer keyboard, provides a comfortable position for her hands when typing. Small sponge rubber sleeves placed on her pens and pencils improve her grasp and facilitate writing. An electric stapler, an electric hole punch, and an automatic letter opener further reduce additional trauma to her wrists.

Elaine has returned to the packing room on a modified schedule, giving her the opportunity to work at a reduced speed and to take more breaks. She finds that wearing a padded glove enables her to grasp the bundles of shades more easily. The height of the packing table has been adjusted, requiring less exertion to lift, carry, and pack the bundles. Elaine's co-workers, eager to prevent injuries from their own repetitive motion, find these adaptations helpful as well.

The cost of the assistive devices and the occupational therapist's fees for several hours of consultation have been inexpensive, far less expensive than training a new employee and placing Elaine on disability insurance.

ORGANIZATIONS

<u>Administration on Aging</u> (AoA)
U. S. Department of Health and Human Services
200 Independence Avenue, SW
Washington, DC 20201
(202) 619-0724   FAX (202) 357-3555   www.aoa.dhhs.gov

A federal agency that acts as an advocate for elders within the federal government. Administers grants, sponsors research, and prepares and disseminates information related to problems of elders, including programs related to employment. Provides technical assistance to state and area agencies on aging. Ten regional offices are listed on the web site.

<u>American Association of Retired Persons</u> (AARP)
601 E Street, NW
Washington, DC 20049
(800) 441-2277   (202) 434-2277   www.aarp.org/scsep

Participates in the federally sponsored Senior Community Service Employment Program (SCSEP) and publishes information about recruiting, training, and managing older workers. Web site has information for older job seekers, including writing resumes and coping with job interviews.

<u>Employment and Training Administration</u> (ETA)
U.S. Department of Labor
200 Constitution Avenue, NW
Washington, DC 20210
(877) 872-5627   www.doleta.gov

Responsible for administering the Senior Community Service Program that employs eligible seniors in part-time jobs.

<u>Equal Employment Opportunity Commission</u> (EEOC)
1801 L Street, NW
Washington, DC 20507
(800) 669-3362 to order publications
(800) 669-4000 to speak to an investigator
(800) 800-68203302 (TTY)
In the Washington, DC metropolitan area, (202) 663-4900
(202) 663-4494 (TTY)   www.eeoc.gov

Responsible for developing and enforcing regulations for the employment section of the Americans with Disabilities Act and the Age Discrimination in Employment Act. Complaints may be filed with the nearest local office, or contact the main office, listed above. Information on filing a complaint is available on the web site. Copies of EEOC regulations are available in standard print, alternate formats, and on the web site. Produces manuals, guidelines, and texts of the laws. Free

National Clearinghouse on State and Local Older Worker Programs
National Association of State Units on Aging
1201 15th Street, NW, Suite 350
Washington, DC 20005
(202) 898-2578   FAX (202) 898-2583   cwellons@nasua.org
www.nasua.org

A source of information on policies and programs for older workers. Conducts on-site training for employers and publishes resource materials.

National Council on Aging (NCOA)
300 D Street, SW, Suite 801
Washington, DC 20024
(800) 424-9046   (202) 479-1200
FAX (202) 479-0735   info@ncoa.org   www.ncoa.org

Participates in the federally sponsored Senior Community Service Employment Program (SCSEP). One of NCOA's constituency groups, the National Older Worker Partnership, serves as an advocate for older workers.

Projects with Industry (PWI)
Office of Special Education and Rehabilitation Services (OSERS)
U.S. Department of Education
400 Maryland Avenue, SW, Room 3332
Washington, DC 20202-2740
(202) 205-8922   FAX (202) 260-9424   lavanna.weems@ed.gov
www.ed.gov/programs/rsapwi/index.html

A federally funded program authorized under the Rehabilitation Act, PWI funds programs that expand job opportunities for individuals with disabilities. Services include training, support, job development, and job placement. One priority within this program is the expansion of services for workers who are age 45 or older and who have disabilities.

Age Discrimination in Employment Law
by Barbara T. Lindemann and David D. Kadue
BNA Books
PO Box 7814
Edison, NJ 0881807814
(800) 960-1220   FAX (732) 346-1624   books@bna.com
www.bnabooks.com

Written by two attorneys, this book describes employment rights under the law and examines issues practitioners confront regarding age discrimination litigation. Discusses who is protected, hiring practices, and mandatory retirement. Includes case citations. $275.00

Age Discrimination in the American Workplace
by Raymond F. Gregory
Rutgers University Press
100 Joyce Kilmer Avenue
Piscataway, NJ 08854
(800) 446-9323   FAX (888)471-9014
booksales@rci.rutgers.edu   rutgerspress.rutgers.edu

This book describes the many forms of discrimination that older workers face in the American workforce. Discusses how to file and substantiate a discrimination claim. $29.95

Aging and Rehabilitation
by Stanley J. Brody and George E. Ruff (eds.)
Springer Publishing Company, New York, NY

A collection of articles written by a multidisciplinary group of authors who suggest practical interventions for common problems, including environmental adaptations and nutrition therapy. Out of print

Ageline
American Association of Retired Persons (AARP)
601 E Street, NW
Washington, DC 20049
(800) 441-2277   (202) 434-2277   www.aarp.org

A bibliographic database that provides citations and abstracts on social, psychological, economic, political, and health issues related to aging. Available through online services and on CD-ROM.

How to Recruit Older Workers
How to Train Older Workers
How to Manage Older Workers
American Association of Retired Persons (AARP)   sending copies
601 E Street, NW
Washington, DC 20049
(800) 441-2277   (202) 434-2277   www.aarp.org

These brochures assist employers in attracting and retaining older workers. Single copies, free.

National Institute on Aging Publications List
National Institute on Aging Information Center
PO Box 8057
Gaithersburg, MD 20898-8057
(800) 222-2225   (800) 222-4225 (TTY)   (301) 587-2528
www.niapublications.org

Describes the publications that are available from NIA for professionals and the public. "Age Page," a series of fact sheets about a variety of issues related to aging, is also available from the same address. Free. "Resource Directory for Older People" lists national and state agencies that provide services to elders. Available in print and as a searchable database on the web site. Free

Recognizing Age Discrimination in Employment
American Association of Retired Persons (AARP)
601 E Street, NW
Washington, DC 20049
(800) 441-2277   (202) 434-2277   www.aarp.org

This publication discusses how to recognize age discrimination and the mandates of the Age Discrimination in Employment Act and how to file a complaint.

Resources for Elders with Disabilities
Resources for Rehabilitation
22 Bonad Road
Winchester, Massachusetts 01890
(781) 368-9094   FAX (781) 368-9096   info@rfr.org
www.rfr.org

A large print resource guide that describes services and products that help elders with disabilities to function independently. Includes chapters on hearing loss, stroke, vision loss, arthritis, diabetes, Parkinson's disease, and osteoporosis. $51.95   (See order form on last page of this book.)

Chapter 7

EMPLOYEES WITH CHRONIC CONDITIONS

The term chronic condition has been applied to a wide variety of illnesses and health conditions, including diabetes, epilepsy, multiple sclerosis, hypertension, and heart conditions. The common feature of chronic conditions is that they are not amenable to medical cure. They vary, however, in their effects and intensity. While some extreme cases of chronic conditions may be life threatening, in many cases individuals are able to carry out the activities of everyday living and working most of the time. Many of these conditions have periods of flare-ups of illness and debilitation, followed by recovery. It is virtually impossible to predict when the flare-ups will occur, causing the individuals to live with a great deal of uncertainty. Some conditions may cause functional limitations, while others may cause fatigue, depression, or no evident symptoms at all.

Chronic conditions may cause a great deal of stress for individuals, especially upon first hearing the diagnosis. It is often difficult for individuals to accept the fact that they will always live with the condition. Learning about resources available to help them cope with the condition and control it to the maximum extent possible may facilitate the adjustment process. Some conditions require that the affected individuals modify their lifestyles through changes in diet, exercise, or the use of medication. Because employees spend so much of their time at the workplace, it is crucial that managers and supervisors understand the condition and how it is likely to affect the work routine, if at all.

Occupational health nurses and physicians can help employees with chronic conditions by providing appropriate referrals and educational materials. They can also offer all employees screenings to detect chronic conditions and provide appropriate medical management in order to prevent a severe episode (Moore and Childre: 1990). Additional services may be available through Employee Assistance Programs (EAP's) offered by many businesses and industries. EAP's can help employees with chronic conditions with medical needs, financial planning, health and disability insurance, and relationships with colleagues. They may also provide counseling regarding job retention and the effects of role reversals in family life.

When the condition causes a functional limitation, the employee may be eligible for services from the state vocational rehabilitation agency. Employees with chronic conditions are covered by the Americans with Disabilities Act, which requires reasonable accommodations on the part of the employer (see Chapter 2, "Federal Laws and Programs").

Although each individual case requires different accommodations, there are some general rules of thumb for employers to consider. Each individual knows his or her own condition the best and should inform the employer if special schedules or facilities are necessary. For example, employees with diabetes may need to have insulin injections and their meals on a schedule. Flexible scheduling of breaks and lunch periods is a logical solution. Making certain that the employee has privacy to inject insulin is also important.

Employees with chronic conditions may need extra time to schedule doctors' appointments. Supervisors and employees should allow for an arrangement that causes minimal disruption to the work schedule. For example, employees may be permitted to use vacation time or a combination of lunch and break periods, or they may be able to work extra hours on another occasion. Similarly, employees who tire easily may be allowed to take naps but may make up the time by working longer or, if possible, by taking work home.

Employees who use personal computers in their work and who have compatible equipment at home may be able to work out an arrangement with the employer to complete certain portions of their work at home. In some cases, it may be helpful to transfer the employee to a position that is less physically demanding or that causes less mental stress.

Although there are many chronic conditions that affect employees, diabetes and epilepsy are conditions which are not only common but have symptoms that can occur without warning. The sections below provide information about how to recognize and provide first aid for an insulin reaction and for an epileptic seizure. (For information about the conditions themselves, see Resources for People with Disabilities and Chronic Conditions, described on page 207 of this book.) As the drug treatment for HIV/AIDS has become more effective, individuals with the virus are now surviving longer and in many cases feeling well enough to carry out normal activities of everyday life, including work. Since HIV/AIDS must now be treated as a chronic disease and is becoming more common in the workplace, a section below deals with this condition in the workplace. (For information about HIV/AIDS itself, see A Mans Guide to Coping with Disability, described on page 205 of this book.)

HOW TO RECOGNIZE AN INSULIN REACTION AND GIVE FIRST AID

Diabetes has become an increasingly prevalent condition in the United States, affecting 6% of the adult population in 2002 (National Center for Health Statistics: 2003). It is a condition where the body is unable to maintain normal blood glucose levels. *Hypoglycemia* is a condition where the level of glucose is too low; *hyperglycemia* is a condition where the level of glucose is too high. Hypoglycemia may lead to an insulin reaction; symptoms include feeling shaky or sweaty, headache, hunger, irritability, and dizziness. Insulin shock sometimes occurs if an insulin reaction is not treated quickly; in these instances, individuals may lose consciousness.

Suggestions for giving first aid to individuals who have had an insulin reaction are:

• Give the individual some food, such as orange juice, milk, or even sugar itself, to replace the low blood sugar level. Many individuals with diabetes carry glucose tablets, sugar packets, or candy with them for use in emergencies.

• If the individual is unconscious, rub honey or another sugary substance into the mouth, between the teeth and cheek.

FIRST AID FOR AN EPILEPTIC SEIZURE

The Epilepsy Foundation reports that accidents and absenteeism are no more frequent among employees with epilepsy than among other employees, although a small group of

102

employees with epilepsy may have an increased risk of accidents (Hauser and Hesdorffer: 1990). Although unpredictable seizures are hazardous in certain environments, when employers and employees are aware of the proper responses, the hazards can be minimized. Epileptic seizures have been mistakenly identified as heart attacks, drunkenness, and drug overdoses. It is important for employers and employees, rehabilitation professionals, and the general public to recognize epileptic seizures and to know simple first aid for epilepsy. A vocational evaluation by a specialist such as an occupational physician can help employees with epilepsy minimize hazards and alleviate the concerns of employers (Floyd et al.: 1988; Roessler et al.: 1990).

If a co-worker appears to having a seizure, check to see if the individual is wearing an identification bracelet or necklace or carrying an identification card which states that he or she has epilepsy.

- Remove hard or sharp items that are in the vicinity of the individual having a seizure.

- Loosen the individual's tie or collar to make breathing easier.

- Place a flat, soft cushion, folded jacket, or sweater under the individual's head.

- Gently turn the individual's head to the side to help keep the airway clear. Never try to place any object between the teeth of an individual experiencing a seizure.

- Do not try to stop the individual's jerking movements.

- Remain with the individual until the seizure ends and offer assistance, if needed.

- If the individual seems confused, offer to call a friend, family member, or taxi to help him/her get home.

- If the seizure continues for more than five minutes; if another seizure begins shortly after the first; or if the individual does not regain consciousness after the jerking movements have ceased, call an ambulance.

- If the individual is having an absence seizure, he or she may have a dazed appearance; stare into space; or exhibit automatic behavior such as shaking an arm or a leg. Speak quietly and calmly and move the person away from any dangerous areas, such as a flight of stairs or a stove. Remain with the individual until consciousness returns.

Individuals whose seizures are under control have no restrictions on most of their activities, although the lack of a driver's license can be a significant barrier to employment. In most states, an individual must be free of seizures for six months to one year in order to be eligible for a driver's license. A letter from a physician which states that seizures are under control may be required.

HIV/AIDS

About three-quarters of all cases of AIDS occur among individuals aged 25 to 44; this is the same group that comprises most of the work force (Centers for Disease Control and Prevention: no date). Their entry or re-entry into the workplace raises many issues, including confronting the fears and negative attitudes of co-workers. A Supreme Court ruling (Supreme Court of the United States: 1998) decided that individuals with HIV/AIDS are covered under the provisions of the Americans with Disabilities Act even if their condition is not yet symptomatic.

It is important to educate co-workers, who may fear that they can become infected by being in close contact with individuals who have the virus. HIV/AIDS is transmitted through the transfer of body fluids such as semen and blood. Sexual intercourse accounts for the greatest proportion of infections, especially among gay men who have anal intercourse with other men. Infection via heterosexual intercourse is also possible. Intravenous drug users who share needles and other drug paraphernalia are also susceptible to infection with HIV, as infected blood that remains on the needle is injected into the user's bloodstream. There are no known cases of HIV transmitted via saliva, tears, or sweat. Since many individuals with HIV/AIDS are homosexual, it is also important to deal with co-workers' negative attitudes toward diverse sexual orientations.

Many employers have developed written policy guidelines for accommodating employees with disabilities and chronic conditions, and some have specific guidelines regarding employees with HIV/AIDS. Employers may need to make accommodations for workers with HIV/AIDS by providing flexible schedules to ensure ample time for appointments with physicians. Other options include part-time positions or job sharing. All health care settings where workers may be exposed to the bodily fluids of patients with HIV/AIDS must have in effect guidelines to prevent the spread of the infection.

The federal government provides a great deal of assistance to employers, employees, labor leaders, and family members through the CDC National AIDS Clearinghouse and the CDC Business and Labor Resource Service (see "ORGANIZATIONS" section below). Assistance with the development of workplace policies, a vast literature on HIV/AIDS in the workplace, and referrals for assistance are all available.

References

Centers for Disease Control and Prevention
no date Accommodating Employees with HIV/AIDS Business Responds to AIDS

Floyd, Michael, John Chaplin, Michael Espir, and Zarrina Kurtz
1988   "The Management of Epilepsy at Work" International Journal of Rehabilitation
        Research 11:1:3-10
Hauser, W. Allen and Dale C. Hesdorffer
1990   Facts about Epilepsy Landover, MD: Epilepsy Foundation of America
Moore, Pamela V. and Frances Childre
1990   "Creative Policy-Making: Strategies for Working with the Healthy Chronically
        Diseased Employee" American Association of Occupational Health Nurses Journal
        38(June):6:284-288
National Center for Health Statistics
2003   Health, United States 2003 Hyattsville, MD
Roessler, Richard T., Kay Fletcher Schriner, and Jim Troxell
1990   "Setting an Employment Agenda: A Demonstration with the Epilepsy Foundation of
        America" Journal of Disability Policy Studies 1(Fall)3:38-51
Supreme Court of the United States
1998   Bragdon v. Abbott et al. No. 97-156 Decided June 25

ORGANIZATIONS

American Diabetes Association (ADA)
1701 North Beauregard Street
Alexandria, VA 22311
(800) 342-2383   In the Washington area, DC, (703) 549-1500
FAX (703) 836-7439   askADA@diabetes.org
www.diabetes.org

National membership organization with local affiliates. Publications for both professionals and consumers, including cookbooks and guides for the management of diabetes (see "PUBLIC-ATIONS AND TAPES" section below). Membership, individuals, $28.00, includes discounts on publications, a subscription to "Diabetes Forecast," which includes articles relevant to individuals with diabetes and family members. The annual "Resource Guide for Diabetes Supplies," which has information about special diabetes products and vendors, is also included in the membership. Membership in a local affiliate is also included. Many local affiliates offer their own publications, sponsor support groups, and conduct professional training programs.

American Heart Association
7272 Greenville Avenue
Dallas, TX 75231-4596
(800) 242-8721   (214) 373-6300   FAX (214) 706-1341
www.americanheart.org

Promotes research and education and publishes professional and public education brochures about heart disease and related conditions such as hypertension and stroke. Local affiliates. Membership fees vary.

CDC Business Responds to AIDS and Labor Responds to AIDS
PO Box 6003
Rockville, MD 20849-6003
(800) 458-5231   (301) 562-1098   (800) 243-7012 (TTY)
FAX (888) 282-7681   hivatwork@cdcnpin.gov   www.brta-lrta.org
www.hivatwork.org

This organization assists business and labor in the development of workplace policies regarding HIV/AIDS through referrals, assistance, and information dissemination. Web site has many publications that may be downloaded, resources, and links. Many of the publications are free, and some are available in Spanish.

CDC National AIDS Hotline
(800) 342-2437   (800) 344-7432 (Spanish)   (800) 243-7889 (TTY)
www.ashastd.org/nah

A 24 hour hotline that provides information about HIV transmission and prevention, HIV testing and treatment, referrals, and educational materials. Special resources are available for minorities. Spanish information specialists are available 8:00 a.m. to 2:00 a.m. E.S.T. and a Spanish recording is available from 2:00 a.m. to 8:00 a.m. E.S.T. The Centers for Disease Control and Prevention (CDC) monitors the HIV/AIDS epidemic and promotes the public understanding of the disease as well as prevention of high risk behavior among students and adults.

Epilepsy Foundation (EF)
4351 Garden City Drive, Suite 406
Landover, MD 20785-2267
(800) 332-1000 Answer line   (800) 213-5821 membership and publications
(301) 459-3700   FAX (301) 577-2684
postmaster@efa.org   www.epilepsyfoundation.org

Provides information and education, advocacy, research support, and services to individuals with epilepsy, their family members, and professionals. Local affiliates. Some publications and audio-visual materials are available in Spanish. Membership, $25.00, includes 10% discount on publications and videotapes, access to mail order pharmacy service, and monthly newsletter, "EpilepsyUSA." Sponsors a Career Support Center, which helps individuals with epilepsy find suitable employment through guides on job preparation, interview preparation, and talking with others in similar situations. Other features on the web site also provide information from experts who answer individual questions.

Food and Drug Administration (FDA)
Office of Special Health Issues
5600 Fishers Lane, HF-12, Room 9-49
Rockville, MD 20857
(301) 827-4460   FAX (301) 443-4555
oshi@oc.fda.gov   www.fda.gov/oashi/aids/hiv.html

Provides information about clinical trials and drugs approved for the treatment of AIDS and problems encountered in the manufacturing process, etc. Provides Internet links to other web sites with information about therapy for AIDS. E-mail listserv provides information on products and meetings.

National AIDS Fund
1030 15th Street, NW, Suite 860
Washington, DC 20005
(888) 234-2437   info@aidsfund.org   www.aidsfund.org

Provides consulting, education, and publications related to HIV/AIDS in the workplace. Many publications available on the web site. Operates the "Return-to-Work Initiative" which has the goals of helping individuals with HIV/AIDS return to work and helping employers integrate returning employees successfully into the workplace.

National Easter Seals Society
230 West Monroe Street, Suite 1800
Chicago, IL 60606-4802
(800) 221-6827   (312) 726-6200   (312) 726-4258 (TTY)
FAX (312) 726-1494   info@easter-seals.org
www.easter-seals.org

Promotes research, education, and rehabilitation for people with physical disabilities, speech and language problems, and chronic conditions; their families; and professionals. Local affiliates.

National Multiple Sclerosis Society
733 Third Avenue
New York, NY 10017-3288
(212) 986-3240   FAX (212) 986-7981
(800) 344-4867 Information Resource Center and Library
Nat@nationalmssociety.org   www.nationalmssociety.org

Provides professional and public education and information and referral; supports research. Offers counseling services, physician referrals, advocacy, discount prescription and health care products program, and assistance in obtaining assistive technology. Regional affiliates throughout the U.S. Information Resource Center and Library answers telephone inquiries from 11:00 a.m. to 5:00 p.m. E.S.T., Monday through Thursday. Membership, $25.00, includes large print magazine, "Inside MS," published three times a year. Newsletter also available on the web site. Individuals with multiple sclerosis may receive a courtesy membership if they are unable to pay. The text of past issues is available on the web site. The web site also has information about clinical studies that are recruiting patients.

ADA and People with MS
by Laura Cooper and Nancy Law with Jane Sarnoff
National Multiple Sclerosis Society (See "ORGANIZATIONS" section above)
(212) 986-3240   FAX (212) 986-7981
(800) 344-4867 Information Resource Center and Library
Nat@nationalmssociety.org   www.nationalmssociety.org

This booklet explains how the Americans with Disabilities Act applies to individuals with multiple sclerosis. Large print. Free. Also available on the web site.

The ADA: Questions and Answers about Provisions Affecting Persons with Seizure Disorders
Epilepsy Foundation (EF) (See "ORGANIZATIONS" section above)
(800) 213-5821   FAX (301) 577-9056
www.epilepsyfoundation.org

This pamphlet describes provisions of the Americans with Disabilities Act covering individuals with seizure disorders including medical examinations, drug testing, and benefits. $1.15

American Diabetes Association Complete Guide to Diabetes
American Diabetes Association
Order Fulfillment
PO Box 930850
Atlanta, GA 31193-0850
(800) 232-6733   FAX (404) 442-9742

This book provides information about type 1 and type 2 diabetes, including how to maintain good blood glucose levels, selecting health care providers, and planning an exercise program. $29.95

The Americans with Disabilities Act: A Guide to Provisions Affecting Persons with Seizure Disorders
Epilepsy Foundation (EF) (See "ORGANIZATIONS" section above)
(800) 213-5821   FAX (301) 577-9056
www.epilepsyfoundation.org

This manual guides prospective employers and employees through the ADA's provisions affecting issues such as interviewing, medical examinations, disability benefits, health and life insurance, and job assignments. $10.95

Diabetes Self-Management
PO Box 52890
Boulder, CO 80322-2890
(800) 234-0923

A bimonthly magazine that helps people with diabetes manage their disease. Tips on diet, foot care, medical news, etc. $15.97

Employment Issues and Multiple Sclerosis
by Phillip D. Rumrill
Demos Medical Publishing
386 Park Avenue South, Suite 201
New York, NY 10016
(800) 532-8663   (212) 683-0072
FAX (212) 683-0118   info@demospub.com   www.demosmedpub.com

This book discuss how employment may be affected by multiple sclerosis. Includes information about vocational rehabilitation, job placement and retention, the Americans with Disabilities Act, and other legal issues. $29.95 Orders placed on the Demos web site receive a 15% discount.

Epilepsy: Legal Rights, Legal Issues
Epilepsy Foundation (EF) (See "ORGANIZATIONS" section above)
(800) 213-5821   FAX (301) 577-9056
www.epilepsyfoundation.org

This pamphlet provides an overview of legal issues such as employment, disability benefits, driving, and insurance. $.82

Epilepsy: 199 Answers
by Andrew N. Wilner
Demos Medical Publishing
386 Park Avenue South, Suite 201
New York, NY 10016
(800) 532-8663   (212) 683-0072
FAX (212) 683-0118   info@demospub.com   www.demosmedpub.com

This guide answers patients' questions about the condition, tests, medications, and research and provides information on driving, work, first aid, and safety. Includes a medical history form and seizure calendar. $19.95 Orders placed on the Demos web site receive a 15% discount.

Epilepsy: The Storm Within
Program Development Associates
PO Box 2038
Syracuse, NY 13220-2038
(800) 543-2119   FAX (315) 452-0710   www.pdassoc.com

This videotape discusses the causes and disease process as well as what should and should not be done to help a person who is having a seizure. 28 minutes $149.00

A Field Guide to Type 1 Diabetes
American Diabetes Association (ADA)
Order Fulfillment
PO Box 930850
Atlanta, GA 31193-0850
(800) 232-6733   FAX (404) 442-9742   www.diabetes.org

This book provides an overview of type 1 diabetes, along with information on what types of supplies are necessary, how to correct both high and low blood sugar, and prevention of complications. $14.95

First Aid for Seizures
Epilepsy Foundation (EF) (See "ORGANIZATIONS" section above)
(800) 213-5821   FAX (301) 577-9056
www.epilepsyfoundation.org

Printed in both English and Spanish, this poster gives simple first aid instruction for people experiencing a seizure. $2.26

HIV@Work: Taking Care of Business
Business Responds to AIDS Program
Labor Responds to AIDS Program
Centers for Disease Control and Prevention
PO Box 6003
Rockville, MD 20849-6003
(800) 458-5231   (301) 562-1098   (800) 243-7012 (TTY)
FAX (888) 282-7681   hivatwork@cdcnpin.gov   www.brta-lrta.org
www.hivatwork.org

This videotape helps employers adopt workplace policies and programs related to HIV/AIDS. Provides information about how to implement a prevention program and information about free resources. Free

Information for Employers
National Multiple Sclerosis Society (See "ORGANIZATIONS" section above)
(212) 986-3240   FAX (212) 986-7981
(800) 344-4867   Nat@nationalmssociety.org
www.nationalmssociety.org

This brochure provides basic information for employers of individuals who have multiple sclerosis. Free. Also available on the web site.

Labor Leader's Kit
Manager's Kit
Business Responds to AIDS Program
Labor Responds to AIDS Program
Centers for Disease Control and Prevention
PO Box 6003
Rockville, MD 20849-6003
(800) 458-5231   (301) 562-1098   (800) 243-7012 (TTY)
FAX (888) 282-7681   hivatwork@cdcnpin.gov   www.brta-lrta.org
www.hivatwork.org

These kits help employers develop policy regarding HIV/AIDS in the workplace, worker education, and family education. The kits include resource guides and catalogues. Free. Also available on the web site.

The Legal Rights of Persons with Epilepsy: An Overview of Legal Issues and Laws
Epilepsy Foundation (EF) (See "ORGANIZATIONS" section above)
(800) 213-5821   FAX (301) 577-9056
www.epilepsyfoundation.org

This manual discusses the legal issues and laws that affect individuals with epilepsy, such as health care, education, employment, driving, vocational rehabilitation, criminal justice, and housing. Includes information on the Americans with Disabilities Act. $16.95

Living Well with Epilepsy
by Robert J. Gumnit
Demos Medical Publishing
386 Park Avenue South, Suite 201
New York, NY 10016
(800) 532-8663   (212) 683-0072
FAX (212) 683-0118   info@demospub.com   www.demosmedpub.com

Written for health professionals and individuals with epilepsy, this book discusses diagnosis and management of seizure disorders. $19.95   Orders placed on the Demos web site receive a 15% discount.

Management by Common Sense
Epilepsy Foundation (EF) (See "ORGANIZATIONS" section above)
(800) 213-5821   FAX (301) 577-9056
www.epilepsyfoundation.org

This booklet, written for employers of individuals with epilepsy, describes the condition and discusses issues such as workers' compensation, effects of medication, and reactions of customers or clients. $2.15

Multiple Sclerosis: The Questions You Have, The Answers You Need
by Rosalind Kalb (ed.)
Demos Medical Publishing
386 Park Avenue South, Suite 201
New York, NY 10016
(800) 532-8663   (212) 683-0072
FAX (212) 683-0118   info@demospub.com   www.demosmedpub.com

Written by professionals who care for individuals with multiple sclerosis, this book provides information about living with the condition and answers questions most commonly asked. Topics include neurology, treatment, employment, legal issues, physical and occupational therapy, and psychosocial issues. $39.95   Orders placed on the Demos web site receive a 15% discount.

Multiple Sclerosis: Your Legal Rights
by Lanny Perkins and Sara Perkins
Demos Medical Publishing
386 Park Avenue South, Suite 201
New York, NY 10016
(800) 532-8663   (212) 683-0072
FAX (212) 683-0118   info@demospub.com   www.demosmedpub.com

Describes the medical and legal issues encountered by individuals with multiple sclerosis. Discusses maintaining employment; how to apply for benefits; obtaining medical coverage; and planning for the future. $21.95   Orders placed on the Demos web site receive a 15% discount.

A Place in the Workforce
National Multiple Sclerosis Society (See "ORGANIZATIONS" section above)
(212) 986-3240   FAX (212) 986-7981
(800) 344-4867   Nat@nationalmssociety.org
www.nationalmssociety.org

This reprint from "Inside MS" discusses strategies for obtaining employment. Free. Also available on the web site.

Safety and Seizures: Tips for Living with Seizure Disorders
Epilepsy Foundation (EF) (See "ORGANIZATIONS" section above)
(800) 213-5821   FAX (301) 577-9056
www.epilepsyfoundation.org

This brochure provides suggestions for first aid for seizure and tips for personal, household, workplace, transportation, and recreation safety. $.95

Should I Work?
National Multiple Sclerosis Society (See "ORGANIZATIONS" section above)
(212) 986-3240   FAX (212) 986-7981
(800) 344-4867   Nat@nationalmssociety.org
www.nationalmssociety.org

This brochure encourages individuals recently diagnosed with multiple sclerosis to continue working and suggests strategies to do so. Free. Also available on the web site.

Type 2 Diabetes: Your Healthy Living Guide
American Diabetes Association (ADA)
Order Fulfillment
PO Box 930850
Atlanta, GA 31193-0850
(800) 232-6733   FAX (404) 442-9742   www.diabetes.org

A guidebook that helps people with type 2 diabetes manage their disease through proper diet, exercise, and the safe use of medications. $16.95

Voices from the Workplace
Epilepsy Foundation (EF) (See "ORGANIZATIONS" section above)
(800) 213-5821   FAX (301) 577-9056
www.epilepsyfoundation.org

In this videotape, individuals with epilepsy describe the coping strategies they use in the workplace. 14 minutes. $21.95

What You Should Know about Returning to Work before Talking with Your Disability Provider
by Nancy L. Breuer
National AIDS Fund
1030 15th Street, NW, Suite 860
Washington, DC 20005
(888) 234-2437   info@aidsfund.org   www.aidsfund.org

This booklet provides practical information for people with HIV/AIDS. Includes a medical checklist and information on disability insurance. Free

The Win-Win Approach to Reasonable Accommodations
by Richard T. Roessler and Phillip Rumrill
National Multiple Sclerosis Society (See "ORGANIZATIONS" section above)
(212) 986-3240   FAX (212) 986-7981
(800) 344-4867   Nat@nationalmssociety.org
www.nationalmssociety.org

This booklet describes the provisions of the Americans with Disability Act and how it protects employees with multiple sclerosis. Suggests possible accommodations and strategies for talking with employers. Free. Also available on the web site.

The Workbook: A Self-Study Guide for Job-Seekers with Epilepsy
Epilepsy Foundation (EF) (See "ORGANIZATIONS" section above)
(800) 213-5821   FAX (301) 577-9056
www.epilepsyfoundation.org

This guide emphasizes the skills required for a job search. Includes setting goals and study exercises. Available in English and Spanish. $10.95

Chapter 8

HEARING AND SPEECH IMPAIRMENTS

Less than two-thirds of individuals with hearing disabilities (61.9%) and just over one-third of those with speech disabilities (37.1%) are employed (McNeil: 2001). A major problem for people who are deaf is underemployment. The reasons for underemployment are varied, including lack of access to quality education (Commission on the Education of the Deaf: 1988) and to career or postsecondary education. Often workers who are deaf or hearing impaired have been limited to blue collar positions; they have not been considered for managerial positions, whether they work in blue collar or white collar positions.

Employers have traditionally had negative attitudes toward hiring workers who are deaf (Schein and Delk: 1974), reflecting society's attitudes toward individuals who have disabilities. Despite this negative perception on the part of employers, data from the Rehabilitation Services Administration suggest that individuals who are deaf have high rates of success when they become clients of rehabilitation programs (Schein and Delk: 1974). Laws requiring institutions that receive federal funds to make their facilities accessible to all qualified individuals have resulted in increased postsecondary educational opportunities for students with hearing or speech impairments. Many community colleges, four year colleges, and universities now have special support services for these students.

Although speech impairments are sometimes caused by disease, individuals with profound hearing impairments often have speech impairments as well. Individuals who are deaf or hearing impaired are able to use their voices and their hands for communicating. Individuals who are nonvocal, however, are unable to articulate intelligibly or at all due to diseases that cause paralysis, inability to control muscles (such as cerebral palsy), or brain damage (Baker et al.: 1991). In some cases, these individuals may be able to use the same types of assistive devices as individuals who are deaf or hearing impaired. In other cases, they will need additional adaptations to accommodate for their mobility impairments as well.

To obtain assistance in hiring new employees or making adaptations for current employees, employers should contact the state vocational rehabilitation agency. Many states now have special agencies to serve people who are deaf or hearing impaired. To find out whether your state has an agency of this type, call the information operator for the state government or the state vocational rehabilitation agency.

Prior to assigning an individual who is deaf or who has a hearing or speech impairment to a specific position, a job analysis should be carried out to determine the communication requirements of the position (Cerna: 1990). Taking into account both the tasks required for the position and the assistive technology available to facilitate communication, it must be determined whether the individual is capable of filling the position. If the individual is able to carry out the major aspects of the position but is unable to do other aspects, it is possible to restructure the position by assigning certain tasks to other individuals.

Current employees who have experienced hearing loss may benefit from a referral to one of the many organizations that provide services, products, and self-help groups. Independent agencies and special services at hospitals often offer these services. In addition, many national organizations have branch offices or chapters throughout the country and will make referrals to these local affiliates (see "ORGANIZATIONS" section below).

Employment of workers who are deaf or who have a hearing or speech impairment is facilitated when supervisors and co-workers are educated about the impairments and how to communicate with their colleagues. Staff members should have the opportunity to learn sign language when employees who use this language work at the organization. Courses in sign language are available at some rehabilitation agencies and also through the use of special software packages. It should not be assumed that all individuals who are hearing impaired use sign language, however; employers should ask employees about their preferred mode of communication.

ASSISTIVE DEVICES AND ENVIRONMENTAL ADAPTATIONS

There are many products available to facilitate communication for individuals who are deaf or who have a hearing or a speech impairment. The most common device, the *hearing aid*, has undergone considerable improvement in recent years. However, it is important to understand that even with a hearing aid, the user's hearing is not the same as normal hearing. Because hearing aids amplify sound, they amplify background noises as well as conversation. Therefore, it may be more difficult for a person who uses a hearing aid to understand conversation in a noisy meeting room than in a quiet office.

Teletypewriters (TTYs), also known as text telephones (TTs), or telephone communication devices for the deaf (TDDs), transmit printed messages across telephone lines. They utilize computers with screens, keyboards, and modems, which serve as the communication devices. TTYs are usually dedicated systems, but some are available that utilize personal computers, providing larger keyboards and screens for display. TTYs may only be used when there is a TTY at the other end of the telephone line. TTYs may be integral parts of telephones, or portable models may be attached to any standard telephone. In addition, some public pay telephones are adapted with TTYs and display the international symbol for a TTY. Telephone companies can provide information about installing a TTY. A TTY operator is available for directory assistance and placing credit card, collect, person-to-person, and third party calls. The local telephone directory includes the toll-free number for this service in a section on services for customers with disabilities.

TTYs are useful for employees with profound hearing impairments or those who are unable to speak. TTYs should be available not only to employees who are deaf or who have a hearing or speech impairment, but also to supervisors and other employees who communicate with them. Options for TTYs include printers; answering machines; speech output that uses a synthetic voice to transmit the typed message; and compatibility with computers. TTYs may be purchased in retail stores that sell telephone equipment and from vendors of special equipment for people who are deaf or hearing impaired (see "VENDORS OF ASSISTIVE DEVICES" section below).

Many businesses now have special TTY numbers to enable people who are deaf or who have a hearing or speech impairment to place orders, make reservations, and the like; these numbers are usually noted on advertisements. In addition, Telecommunications for the Deaf (see "ORGANIZATIONS" section below) publishes an annual edition of the "International Directory of TDD Users" that lists phone numbers of businesses and individuals who are members of their organization.

The use of *facsimile machines* (fax machines) also facilitates telephone communication for people who are deaf or hearing impaired or nonvocal. Although fax machines permit only one way communication, they are an option for communicating with parties who do not have TTYs since they may only be used when there is a TTY at the other end of the telephone line. However, the Americans with Disabilities Act has mandated that telephone companies provide telephone relay services (TRS) so that individuals may communicate by phone when one party does not have a TTY; there is no additional charge for this service. A communications assistant relays the conversation from text to voice and from voice to text. The Americans with Disabilities Act requires that all common carriers provide nationwide 24-hour telephone relay service. In addition to the relay services provided by telephone companies, the federal government operates the Federal Information Relay Service (FIRS) so that TTY users may communicate with employees in federal agencies who do not have TTYs; the number to call to access the FIRS is (800) 877-8339 (V/TTY).

Telephone amplifiers make communication easier for many individuals with hearing loss. Available in a variety of models, some are easy to use and produce high quality sound, while others are difficult to use and produce inferior sound. Hand-held telephone amplifiers and volume controls attach to phones at home and at work and are useful when traveling. Some states provide telephone amplifiers to qualified users at no charge; the state office that serves individuals who are deaf or hearing impaired should know if the state provides these devices. These devices have become so commonplace that many stores and mail order catalogues that sell phone equipment stock amplifiers as well as TTYs. Federal law in the United States requires that telephones with cords and cordless telephones be compatible with hearing aids. Some individuals with hearing loss use speaker phones to respond to a caller while watching an interpreter translate what the caller is saying.

Employees who are deaf or hearing impaired may use a *tactile pager* with a vibrating signal and a screen displaying a message. Some models can receive messages from touch-tone telephones, TTYs, and computers. Pagers that can be set to give a vibrating signal may be rented or purchased from local paging and signaling equipment services (listed in the Yellow Pages). Special software is used with any keyboard to type the message that goes to the pager. Some devices require a separate telephone line for each tactile pager; others interface with all paging equipment over one telephone line. Distances covered by pagers vary from local to regional to national, depending on arrangements made with the paging equipment company.

Electronic mail (e-mail) enables individuals with hearing and speech impairments to communicate with others at the workplace and all over the world. Using a personal computer and the Internet, individuals may send and receive messages rapidly. Verbal communication is unnecessary to send letters, memos, job postings, and training materials by computer throughout the workplace.

Visual alerting systems are available for use as smoke or fire detectors or to indicate that the phone is ringing. These systems are necessary to alert individuals who are deaf or hearing impaired that they have a phone call and to prevent co-workers from the annoyance of a ringing phone that goes unanswered. A visual fire or smoke alarm will alert employees who are unable to hear an oral alarm. Visual or vibrating alerting systems may be useful for other types of emergencies at the workplace, such as spills of toxic chemicals.

Some individuals who are deaf or hearing impaired use dogs that are trained to lead their owners to the source of sound, such as ringing telephones and doorbells and to potentially dangerous situations. Owners may bring their dogs to their place of employment to help them perform their jobs and maintain a sense of security. Co-workers should be aware of the fact that these dogs are not pets and should be respectful of the instructions the owners give them regarding the dogs.

Devices that enable people with speech impairments to communicate are referred to as *augmentative communication devices*. Communication boards depict symbols that represent words or ideas; people who are unable to speak may point to the symbols to communicate. Speech synthesizers (which are also used by people who are visually impaired or blind) are artificial voices that utilize modern technology; they may be built into a communication board or they may be part of a computer system. When part of a computer system, they may be used with a variety of options, such as printers, keyboards, and headpointers for people with limited mobility. Some speech synthesizers are part of the hardware of a computer system, while others produce speech by using special screen reader software programs. Portable speech amplifiers are available for people who have had laryngectomies. Devices to help people who have had laryngectomies learn to use their esophageal voice and artificial larynxes are also available.

Personal computers with speech synthesizers may be used in conjunction with software programs to train individuals with speech impairments to improve their verbal skills. These programs help with articulation, stuttering, pitch, and rate, and provide evaluative feedback of the individual's speech. Special programs have been developed for impairments caused by various conditions, such as aphasia and brain injury, and for children. Some speech synthesizers connected to computers enable individuals with speech impairments to communicate over the telephone. TTYs may also be used for phone communication by anyone who is unable to speak.

Portable communication aids operate on batteries and enable the user to locate words or phrases that are pronounced by a speech synthesizer. For people who have mobility impairments as well as speech impairments, switches are available to facilitate the use of augmentative communication devices. Different types of switches are designed for operation by different parts of the body. For example, puff switches are activated by blowing into a mouthpiece; others may be operated by the hands or the feet; and some may be mounted on wheelchairs. These devices enable individuals with speech and mobility impairments to utilize speech synthesizers for communication as well as for data entry. (see Chapter 9, "Mobility Impairments"). A system of scanning enables individuals with severe mobility impairments to enter information by pointing to one of several characters, words, or phrases displayed on a monitor. An alternative way of scanning is to use eye movements. Using switches and pointers may result in a very slow entry of data. Attempts to increase the speed of data entry include the use of Morse code and abbreviations.

In addition to providing special equipment, employers should take measures to ensure that employees who are deaf or hearing impaired are able to understand the discussions that take place at business meetings and social interactions of employees. This sometimes means hiring an interpreter, if only for special meetings, training programs, and large group situations. When an interpreter is present, all statements and questions should be addressed to the person who is deaf or hearing impaired and not to the interpreter. The state vocational rehabilitation agency, a state agency for individuals who are deaf or hearing impaired, or the Registry for Interpreters of the Deaf (see "ORGANIZATIONS" section below) can provide a list of interpreters. State agencies provide interpreters at no cost under certain specified conditions.

In some cases, employees are able to combine the use of a hearing aid and speechreading to understand a discussion. Speechreading, sometimes called lipreading, is a supportive visual process that assists in understanding language. Speakers should make certain that their faces are always turned toward the audience and that they do not cover their lips with their hands or other objects. Because many consonants appear as similar mouth shapes, it is impossible to decipher most of spoken English through speechreading alone.

Background noises should be eliminated to the maximum extent possible. Individuals who wear hearing aids often are unable to understand speech, because background noises that are amplified by their hearing aid interfere. Selection of heating systems and air conditioners as well as other pieces of equipment should take into account the level of noise that they produce. Curtains and carpets contribute to good acoustics by absorbing background noise. Furniture should be placed so that small groups of employees sitting together are close enough to speechread.

Interpreted captioning is a system that enables people with hearing loss who are not fluent in sign language or speechreading to understand the conversation at group meetings (Grant and Walsh: 1990). There are several methods of interpreted captioning. In visual recording, a volunteer uses large sheets of paper to record the meeting in words, symbols, and graphics. In real time captioning, an operator types the dialogue from a meeting into a computer. The computer display may be presented in enlarged form by projection onto a screen or wall; alternatively, large print software used with a video monitor may be sufficient to enable members of the group to read the proceedings. Live captioning is produced by obtaining an advanced copy of the lecture and playing it on a video monitor simultaneously with the lecture presentation.

Some individuals will benefit from the installation of assistive listening devices. These devices transmit sound waves from microphones used by the speaker directly into the ears of individuals with hearing loss. Infrared and FM assistive listening devices are useful for group situations. These devices should be installed in auditoriums and other rooms that are frequently used for group meetings.

Because individuals who are deaf or hearing impaired rely on visual cues to communicate, the workplace should be designed to make these cues as visible as possible. Good lighting, the elimination of glare, and high quality graphics enhance visual cues. Warning signs, peepholes, and window panels in doors will enhance safety as well.

Case Vignette

Peter Duggan, A Financial Analyst with Severe Hearing Impairment

Peter Duggan is 23 years old and recently graduated from a well respected college with a bachelor's degree in business administration. Peter made the Dean's list throughout his four years at college and is now eagerly anticipating his first job. However, Peter has a severe hearing impairment as a result of spinal meningitis that he experienced as a small child. Although Peter was successful as a "mainstreamed" student throughout his education, he is aware of the lack of employment opportunities for individuals who are deaf or hearing impaired. For this reason, he decided to use the services of the state vocational rehabilitation agency in his search for employment.

Mary Stapleton, the vocational rehabilitation counselor, obtained Peter's college records and recommendations from several professors in the field of business administration. It was apparent to Mary that Peter would make an excellent employee, based on his high grades and conscientious work habits. However, Mary had no knowledge of available positions in the field of financial analysis. Therefore, she referred Peter to the local Projects with Industry program, which actively conducted outreach programs for human resource professionals at local businesses.

Peter's records were passed on to the Projects with Industry job placement specialist, Fred Greco. Although Fred did not have a position in mind, he did have contacts with human resource directors at a number of financial companies. After phoning several and describing Peter's qualifications, he learned of a potential entry level position at the First State Financial Security Company. With Peter's permission, Fred made an appointment for Peter to have an employment interview at the company.

Since this was Peter's first venture seeking employment, both he and Fred agreed that it would be a good idea to simulate several interviews so that Peter could practice. With Fred playing the role of the human resources director, Peter had the opportunity to respond to a variety of questions related to the position, his background, and his career goals. Because Peter's speech is very intelligible and his speechreading skills excellent, Fred recommended that Peter

Continued on next page

go to the interview by himself. Peter, however, expressed trepidation about going alone, since this was his first job interview and he feared the possibility that he would not be able to understand the interviewer. As a result, the interpreter from the Projects with Industry staff was assigned to accompany Peter on the interview.

At First State Financial, Peter met with both the human resources director and the division director for financial analysis. Peter provided satisfactory answers to the questions of both interviewers and made a favorable impression. Peter also learned that the company had a policy of reviewing each employee's accomplishments each year and a program to provide further education as an employee benefit. Since Peter hoped to become a manager someday, he felt that this benefit would be extremely important to his continued professional success. At the end of the interviews, the division manager, Patricia Humboldt, told Peter that she would be in touch with him.

Several days later, Peter received a call on his text telephone from Fred Greco at Projects with Industry. Fred relayed the information that Patricia Humboldt had been very impressed with Peter but was concerned about the need to pay for the services of an interpreter in order that Peter interact successfully with his colleagues. Fred had explained to her that Peter had gone all through public school and college and only needed an interpreter on those rare occasions when he could not be guaranteed a seat very close to the speaker. Fred had also informed Patricia that the staff from Projects with Industry would be able to conduct a worksite assessment to determine the environmental modifications and assistive devices that would be necessary and to conduct an educational program for the division staff so that they could understand Peter's needs. Since Projects with Industry is federally funded, these services would be conducted at no cost to the company. Furthermore, since all employees at First State Financial are hired on a six month probationary period, Peter could have the same chance as all other employees to prove his worth to the company. Patricia agreed that these suggestions were reasonable, and she and Fred set up a time for Peter to return for a worksite assessment.

Peter's computer system for carrying out his financial analysis would be the same as those of his colleagues. The system enables company employees at different offices throughout the country to communicate by E-mail. For communication with those who do not participate in E-mail, Peter would need a text telephone that enables him to type out his part of a conversation. When the

Continued on next page

conversation is with another party who also has a text telephone, the communication is carried out independently. When the other party does not have a text telephone, an operator known as a communications assistant provided by the phone company transcribes the typed text to speech and vice versa. In addition to the text telephone, Peter would need a visual alerting system to indicate when his phone was ringing.

During the worksite assessment, the rooms where staff meetings were normally held were evaluated for optimal seating arrangement as well as the possibility of installing an assistive listening device. Since the room was small and the meetings informal, Peter decided that he would not need such a device. Should it be necessary for Peter to attend meetings outside the company in an unknown setting, the state vocational rehabilitation agency would provide an interpreter.

A staff member from the Project with Industry arranged to conduct a session for Peter's supervisor and co-workers so that they could understand his special needs and how to communicate with Peter. Peter was present at the session to answer questions and to help his co-workers feel comfortable with him. The causes of hearing impairment and deafness, sign language, the variety of assistive devices available, and potentially hazardous situations were discussed. The person with whom Peter would share an office was assigned the responsibility of alerting Peter if a fire or other emergency situation occurred; in addition, a visual alerting alarm system would be installed.

Peter began his new position knowing that he had an advocate at the Projects with Industry. Although he felt confident that he would be able to carry out the responsibilities of the position without additional assistance, he appreciated the fact that Projects with Industry remained in contact with the employee and employer during the first year of employment. This arrangement also helped his supervisor feel comfortable that she would be able to find assistance should any unusual problems arise.

The following suggestions will facilitate communications and help co-workers feel more comfortable. At the same time, the employee who has the disability will know that colleagues care enough to take these small but significant measures:

• Be certain that the person knows that you are speaking to him or her. Identify yourself (e.g., point to your name badge).

• Always face the person throughout the conversation so that he or she may get visual cues. Be certain that your mouth is visible throughout the conversation, even if the person with hearing loss is not an experienced speechreader.

• Eliminate background noises to the maximum extent possible.

• Speak clearly at a level just slightly above normal, but do not shout.

• If the person does not understand what you are saying, re-phrase the sentence. Ask the person if he or she has understood you. Similarly, if you do not understand the person with a hearing or speech impairment, ask the individual to repeat what he or she has said. Writing notes is an acceptable means of communication when verbal exchanges are not understood.

• If the need arises to discuss personal or personnel issues, arrange to use a private room to avoid eavesdropping by colleagues.

• When speaking to a person through an interpreter, look directly at the person and speak in the same way as you would in any other conversation. Do not say to the interpreter, "Ask *him* or *her*.."

• In group situations, chairs should be placed so that everyone can see the speaker readily. If the room is large, individuals who are deaf or hearing impaired should be seated in a position where they can easily see the speaker's lips.

• Include co-workers who are deaf or who have a hearing or speech impairment in social activities, such as coffee breaks, group lunches, and other organized activities. One of the main complaints these employees have about their work situations (and life in general) is a feeling of social isolation. After working for a while with individuals who have one or more of these disabilities, co-workers should be able to develop a system of communication, using oral speech, signs, and writing notes. The person who uses sign language is usually willing to teach colleagues some basic signs to facilitate communication.

• Install alerting devices that use flashing lights to indicate fire or other emergencies. Assign a nearby co-worker responsibility for making sure that the employee who is deaf or has a hearing impairment is safely evacuated during emergencies.

• If a co-worker stutters, do not finish his or her sentence or offer advice. Wait patiently for the person to finish and maintain eye contact.

• Ask questions that require only short answers or a nod. If you are having difficulty understanding the individual, ask if writing a note is acceptable.

• If the individual is using a communication device, try to move to a quiet or private location without distractions for your conversation.

Individuals who are deaf or have a hearing or speech impairment should have the same opportunity for initial employment and advancement within the organization as all other employees. The accommodations described above should be applied to training opportunities and advanced education programs that are required for upward mobility within the organization and the field.

References

Baker, Bruce R., Robert T. Stump, Eric H. Nyberg, III, and Robert V. Conti
1991   "Augmentative Communication and Vocational Rehabilitation" Vocational Rehabilitation April:71-83
Cerna, Ric
1990   "Job Restructuring and Engineering for Persons with Hearing Impairments" The Connecticut Rehabilitation Engineering Center Newsletter 1(Winter):4:1, 3
Commission on the Education of the Deaf
1988   Toward Equality: Education of the Deaf Washington, D.C.: U.S. Government Printing Office
Grant, Nancy C. and Birrell Walsh
1990   "Interpreted Captioning: Facilitating Interactive Discussion Among Hearing Impaired Adults" International Journal of Technology and Aging 3(Fall/Winter)2:133-144

McNeil, John M.
2001   Americans With Disabilities 1997 Washington, DC: U.S. Bureau of the Census
        Current Population Reports P70-73
Schein, Jerome D. and Marcus T. Delk, Jr.
1974   The Deaf Population of the United States Silver Spring, MD: National Association
        of the Deaf

ORGANIZATIONS

Alexander Graham Bell Association for the Deaf
3417 Volta Place, NW
Washington, DC 20007
(866) 337-5220   (202) 337-5220   (202) 337-5221 (TTY)
FAX (202) 337-8314   info@agbell.org   www.agbell.org

A membership organization that provides resources that help people with hearing loss learn about hearing aids and how to lip-read. Membership, $50.00, includes "Volta Review," a professional journal and "Volta Voices," a magazine. Members receive a 15% discount on prepaid orders of publications.

American Speech-Language-Hearing Association (ASHA)
10801 Rockville Pike
Rockville, MD 20852
(800) 498-2071   (301) 897-5700   (301) 897-0157 (TTY)
FAX (301) 571-0457   actioncenter@asha.org   www.asha.org

A professional organization of speech-language pathologists and audiologists. Provides information on communication problems and a free list of certified audiologists and speech therapists for each state. Also available on the web site. Toll-free Helpline offers answers to questions about conditions and services as well as referrals, (800) 638-8255 (V/TTY).

Association of Late-Deafened Adults (ALDA)
1131 Lake Street, Suite 204
Oak Park, IL 60301
(877) 907-1738 (V/FAX)   (708) 358-0135 (TTY)   www.alda.org

Sponsors a network of self-help groups for adults throughout the U.S. and Canada who became deaf as adults. Provides information and consultations for professionals and the public. Membership, individuals, $20.00; businesses, $40.00; includes quarterly newsletter, "ALDA News."

Gallaudet University
800 Florida Avenue, NE
Washington, DC 20002
(202) 651-5000 (V/TTY)   gallaudet.edu

The recipient of federal funding, Gallaudet is a university for students who are deaf. Classes are taught in sign language, and a wide range of support services are available. Conducts outreach programs through distribution of educational materials developed at Gallaudet, workshops, and seminars. The Gallaudet Research Institute conducts research in areas related to deafness (gri.gallaudet.edu).

International Association of Laryngectomees (IAL)
Box 691060
Stockton, CA 95269-1060
(866) 425-3678   FAX (209) 472-0516   ialhq@larynxlink.com
www.larynxlink.com

Sponsors self-help groups throughout the U.S. and disseminates information through its publications. Newsletter, "IAL News," published three times a year, free. Some back issues available on the web site.

National Aphasia Association (NAA)
29 John Street, Suite 103
New York, NY 10036
(800) 922-4622   (212) 255-4329
FAX (212) 267-2612   naa@aphasia.org
www.aphasia.org

Promotes public awareness, publishes public education brochures, and develops community programs for people with aphasia. Maintains list of health care professionals who will make referrals to local resources. Publishes a variety of inexpensive fact sheets and "Aphasia Community Group Manual," for organizers of local aphasia support groups. $25.00. No membership fee but requests donation of $25.00. Newsletter updates appear on web site.

National Association of the Deaf (NAD)
814 Thayer Avenue
Silver Spring, MD 20910
(301) 587-1788   (301) 587-1789 (TTY)
FAX (301) 587-1791   NADinfo@nad.org www.nad.org

A membership organization with state chapters throughout the U.S. Advocates for its members and serves as an information clearinghouse. Special programs for youths and special sections for senior citizens, federal employees, and sign language instructors. Holds national and regional conventions. Membership, individuals, $40.00; seniors (over 60), $25.00. "Job Market Online" has classified employment ads. Free access. The Law and Advocacy Center (LAC) develops strategies to improve access for individuals who are deaf or hard-of-hearing through litigation and proposed legislation.

National Easter Seals Society
230 West Monroe Street, Suite 1800
Chicago, IL 60606-4802
(800) 221-6827   (312) 726-6200   (312) 726-4258 (TTY)
FAX (312) 726-1494   info@easter-seals.org
www.easter-seals.org

Promotes research, education, and rehabilitation for people with physical disabilities and speech and language problems. Sponsors Easter Seals Stroke Clubs for people who have had strokes, their families, and friends.

National Institute on Deafness and Other Communication Disorders Information Clearinghouse (NIDCD)
1 Communication Avenue
Bethesda, MD 20892
(800) 241-1044   (800) 241-1055 (TTY)   FAX (301) 770-8977
nidcdinfo@nidcd.nih.go   www.nidcd.nih.gov

The NIDCD is a federal agency that funds basic research studies on problems of hearing, balance, voice, language, and speech. The Clearinghouse provides information on health aspects of these diseases for professionals and the public. Provides searchable databases, brochures, and fact sheets, plus a newsletter "Inside NIDCD." Free

National Stroke Association   (NSA)
9707 East Easter Lane
Englewood, CO 80112
(800) 787-6537   (303) 649-9299   (303) 649-0122 (TTY)
FAX (303) 649-1328   www.stroke.org

Assists individuals with stroke and educates their families, physicians, and the general public about stroke. Membership, allied health professionals, $75.00; physicians, $125.00. Quarterly magazine, "Stroke Smart," free for individuals.

National Technical Institute for the Deaf (NTID)
Center on Employment
Rochester Institute of Technology
Lyndon Baines Johnson Building
52 Lomb Memorial Drive
Rochester, NY 14623
(585) 475-6219 (V/TTY)   FAX (585) 475-7570
ntidcoe@rit.edu   www.ntid.rit.edu

A federally funded technical college created for students who are deaf within a larger institution for students with normal hearing. Offers courses in business, allied health, science and engineering, and visual communication. Students may enroll in courses in the other colleges within the Rochester Institute of Technology. Required cooperative work experience often leads to permanent employment for NTID graduates. The Center on Employment helps students prepare for job interviews; conducts seminars on deafness for employers; and conducts in-depth training programs both on campus and across the country for supervisors of people who are deaf. Works with employers who send recruiters to the campus and supplies interpreters, if necessary. Provides assistance and consultation to employers who have hired individuals who are deaf. Conducts periodic workshops, "Climbing the Career Ladder," for professionals who are deaf.

Registry for Interpreters of the Deaf (RID)
333 Commerce Street
Alexandria, VA 22314
(703) 838-0030   (703) 838-0459 (TTY)   FAX (703) 838-0454
608-www.rid.org

RID is the national certifying organization for interpreters. Establishes guidelines for professional interpreters. Produces directory of training programs for interpreters throughout the country. Maintains a list of interpreters (available on the web site) and postsecondary institutions that offer interpreter training programs.

Rehabilitation Engineering and Assistive Technology Society of North America/RESNA
1700 North Moore Street, Suite 1540
Arlington, VA 22209
(703) 524-6686   (703) 524-6639 (TTY)   FAX (703) 524-6630
info@resna.org   www.resna.org

Interdisciplinary membership organization for the advancement of rehabilitation and assistive technology. Special interest groups include augmentative and alternative communication and sensory aids, job accommodation, computer applications, and universal access. Professional specialty groups for manufacturers and suppliers of rehabilitation products, rehabilitation engineers, occupational therapists, and other professionals. Holds an annual conference. Membership, $150.00, includes semi-annual journal, "Assistive Technology," and quarterly "RESNA Newsletter." Subscription to "Assistive Technology" only, individuals, $65.00; institutions, $75.00.

Rehabilitation Engineering Research Center on Hearing Enhancement
Gallaudet University
800 Florida Avenue, NE
Washington, DC 20002-3695
(202) 651-5335 (V/TTY)   matthew.bakke@gallaudet.edu
www.hearingresearch.org

A federally funded center that conducts research to find technological solutions for people who are hearing impaired. Disseminates research results, holds conferences, and conducts training sessions. Publications list available on web site. Some publications also available on web site.

Rehabilitation Research and Training Center on Improving Vocational Rehabilitation for Individuals Who are Deaf or Hard of Hearing
University of Arkansas
4601 West Markham Street
Little Rock, AR 72205
(501) 686-9691 (V/TTY)   FAX (501) 686-9698   dwatson@uark.edu
www.uark.edu/depts/deafrtc

A federally funded research center that focuses on enhancing the transition from school to work for people who are deaf or hearing impaired. Also addresses communication and adjustment skills. Sponsors workshops, conferences, and graduate training programs.

Self Help for Hard of Hearing People (SHHH)
7910 Woodmont Avenue, Suite 1200
Bethesda, MD 20814
(301) 657-2248   (301) 657-2249 (TTY)   FAX (301) 913-9413
webteam@hearingloss.org   www.hearingloss.org

National membership organization with local and regional chapters. Provides information, support, and individual referrals. Provides e-news, chatrooms, and a listserv. Membership, individuals, $25.00; professionals, $50.00; includes subscription to bimonthly magazine, "Hearing Loss: The Journal of Self Help for Hard of Hearing People."

Stroke Connection
American Stroke Association (ASA)
7272 Greenville Avenue
Dallas, TX 75231
(888) 478-7653   www.strokeassociation.org

Coordinates a network of more than 1,200 stroke clubs and groups. "Stroke Information Alliance" is a quarterly e-newsletter with updates on ASA programs and products. "Stroke Connection Magazine" in print or online, free. Many publications available on the web site.

Telecommunications for the Deaf (TDI)
8630 Fenton Street, Suite 604
Silver Spring, MD 20910
(301) 589-3786   (301) 589-3006 (TTY)   FAX (301) 589-3797
info@tdi-online.org   www.tdi-online.org

Membership organization that lobbies for improved telecommunication for individuals who are deaf or hearing impaired. Publishes "National Directory of TDD Users" annually. Membership, $25.00, includes directory listing and newsletter, "GA-SK." "Resource Guide" is a directory of TTy users, information about the internet, and organizations for TTY users; members, $10.00; nonmembers, $20.00.

Trace Research and Development Center
University of Wisconsin-Madison
2107 Engineering Center Building
1550 Engineering Drive
Madison, WI 53706
(608) 262-6966   (608) 263-5408 (TTY)
FAX (608) 262-8848   info@trace.wisc.edu   trace.wisc.edu

Conducts research to make off-the-shelf technology more accessible to individuals with disabilities through universal design.

United Cerebral Palsy Association (UCPA)
1660 L Street, NW, Suite 700
Washington, DC 20036
(800) 872-5827   (202) 776-0406   (202) 973-7197
FAX (202) 776-0414   webmaster@ucpa.org   www.ucpa.org

Member groups throughout the country provide treatment, information, education, and counseling. Web site includes information on selecting augmentative communication systems. UCPA helps job seekers find a job by assisting with preparing a resume, providing career information, and providing job opportunities,

United States Access Board
1331 F Street, NW, Suite 1000
Washington, DC 20004-1111
(800) 872-2253   (800) 993-2822 (TTY)   (202) 272-5434
(202) 272-5449 (TTY)   FAX (202) 272-5447
info@access-board.gov   www.access-board.gov

A federal agency charged with developing standards for accessibility in federal facilities, public accommodations, and transportation facilities as required by the Americans with Disabilities Act and other federal laws. Publishes the "Uniform Federal Accessibility Standards," which describes accessibility standards for buildings and dwelling units developed for four federal agencies. Provides technical assistance, sponsors research, and distributes publications. Developed standards for Section 508 requirements for electronic and information technology. These new guidelines deal primarily with technology for people who are deaf or hearing impaired and discuss the compatibility of telecommunication products with hearing aids, cochlear implants, TTYs, and assistive listening devices. Guidelines available on the web site (www.access-board.gov/508.htm). Publishes free bimonthly newsletter, "Access Currents," available in standard print, alternate formats, via e-mail, and on the web site.

U.S. Society for Augmentative and Alternative Communication (USSAAC)
PO Box 21418
Sarasota, FL 34276
(941) 312-0992   FAX (941) 312-0992
ussaac@comcast.net   www.ussaac org

A membership organization that advocates for augmentative and alternative communication for individuals who do not speak. Conducts public awareness activities; provides information and referrals and professional education. Membership, consumers/families, $32.00; professionals, $63.00; includes quarterly newsletter, "Speak Up."

Assistive Listening Systems
United States Access Board
1331 F Street, NW, Suite 1000
Washington, DC 20004-1111
(800) 872-2253   (800) 993-2822 (TTY)   (202) 272-5434
(202) 272-5449 (TTY)   FAX (202) 272-5447
www.access-board.gov

Describes the various types of assistive listening systems. Free. Also available on the web site.

Augmentative and Alternative Communication
by David R. Beukelman and Pat Mirenda
Brookes Publishing Company
PO Box 10624
Baltimore, MD 21285-9945
(800) 638-3775   FAX (410) 337-8539
custserv@pbrookes.com   www.brookespublishing.com

This book discusses the communication needs of children and adults with disabilities and methods of implementing augmentative and alternative communication. $59.95

College and Career Programs for Deaf Students
Gallaudet Research Institute
800 Florida Avenue, NE
Attention: dissemination Office
Washington, DC 20002-3660
(800) 451-8834, ext. 5575 (V/TTY)
(202) 651-5575 (V/TTY)   FAX (202) 651-5746
gri.gallaudet.edu

This publication describes admissions, costs, degrees granted, and support services for deaf students at postsecondary programs throughout the U.S. $12.95

Communicating with the Deaf
Films for the Humanities and Sciences
PO Box 2053
Princeton, NJ 08543-2053
(800) 257-5126   FAX (609) 671-0266
custserv@films.com   www.films.com

This videotape provides instructions and strategies to improve communication between people with normal hearing and those who are deaf or hearing impaired. 34 minutes $99,95

The Consumers Guide to Hearing Aids
Self Help for Hard of Hearing People (SHHH)
7910 Woodmont Avenue, Suite 1200
Bethesda, MD 20814
(301) 657-2248   (301) 657-2249 (TTY)   FAX (301) 913-9413
webteam@hearingloss.org   www.hearingloss.org

This booklet describes the different styles, models, and features of hearing aids. Compares the various types of aids. Includes a glossary. $5.50

The EASE Program
Telecommunications for the Deaf (TDI)
8630 Fenton Street, Suite 604
Silver Spring, MD 20910
(301) 589-3786   (301) 589-3006 (TTY)   FAX (301) 589-3797
info@tdi-online.org   www.tdi-online.org

This training program prepares emergency service providers to handle calls from people who use TTYs and to comply with the Americans with Disabilities Act. $35.00

Enhancing the Employability of Deaf Persons
by Steven E. Boone and Gregory A. Long (eds.)
Charles C. Thomas Publisher, Springfield

This book describes a model project developed by the Arkansas Rehabilitation and Training Center to improve the employment capabilities of people who are deaf. Describes goal setting for trainees, career education, assertiveness training, and skills training. Out of print

Implementing the Americans with Disabilities Act: Working Effectively with Persons Who are Deaf or Hard of Hearing
Rehabilitation Research and Training Center for Persons Who Are Deaf or Hard of Hearing
University of Arkansas
4601 West Markham Street
Little Rock, AR 72205
(501) 686-9691 (V/TTY)   FAX (501) 686-9698
rehabres@cavern.uark.edu   www.uark.edu/depts/deafrtc

This publication describes the job accommodations that help people who are hearing impaired or deaf, how to improve communications with individuals with normal hearing, and how to enhance job productivity. Free. Available on the web site.

Journal of Rehabilitation Research and Development (JRRD)
Scientific and Technical Publications Section
Rehabilitation Research and Development Service
103 South Gay Street
Baltimore, MD 21202
(410) 962-1800   FAX (410) 962-9670   pubs@vard.org
www.vard.org

A bimonthly publication of scientific and engineering articles including those related to augmentative communication devices. Free

Legal Rights: The Guide for Deaf and Hard of Hearing People
Gallaudet University Press
Chicago Distribution Center
11030 South Langley Avenue
(800) 621-2736   (888) 630-9347 (TTY)   FAX (800) 621-8476
gupress.gallaudet.edu

This book discusses the legal rights of people with hearing impairments in situations such as employment, education, and health care. Federal and state statutes included. $29.95

Living with Hearing Loss
by Marcia B. Dugan
Self Help for Hard of Hearing People (SHHH)
7910 Woodmont Avenue, Suite 1200
Bethesda, MD 20814
(301) 657-2248   (301) 657-2249 (TTY)   FAX (301) 913-9413
webteam@hearingloss.org   www.hearingloss.org

This book discusses the types and causes of hearing loss; professional evaluations; hearing aids; assistive technology; and tips for communications. $11.95

Managing Employer Development: A Trainer's Manual
Rehabilitation Research and Training Center for Persons Who Are Deaf or Hard of Hearing
University of Arkansas
4601 West Markham Street
Little Rock, AR 72205
(501) 686-9691 (V/TTY)   FAX (501) 686-9698
rehabres@cavern.uark.edu   www.uark.edu/depts/deafrtc

A publication and videotape designed to enhance the employment of people who are deaf through organized employer contacts and follow-ups. $30.00

NIDCD Information Resource Directory
National Institute on Deafness and Other Communication Disorders Information Clearinghouse (NIDCD)
1 Communication Avenue
Bethesda, MD 20892
(800) 241-1044   (800) 241-1055 (TTY)   FAX (301) 770-8977
nidcdinfo@nidcd.nih.go   www.nidcd.nih.gov

This annual directory describers organizations that deal with hearing, balance, smell, taste, voice, speech,and language. Free. Also available on the web site. updates are made on the web site version, www.nidcd.nih.gov/resdir/resource.html.

Resources for People with Disabilities and Chronic Conditions
Resources for Rehabilitation
22 Bonad Road
Winchester, Massachusetts 01890
(781) 368-9094   FAX (781) 368-9096   info@rfr.org
www.rfr.org

A comprehensive resource guide with chapters on hearing and speech impairments, spinal cord injuries, low back pain, diabetes, multiple sclerosis, Parkinson's disease, vision impairment and blindness, and epilepsy. Includes information about the disease or condition; psychological aspects of the condition; professional service providers; environmental adaptations; assistive devices; and descriptions of organizations, publications, and products. $56.95. (See order form on last page of this book.)

Sound Advice on Hearing Aids
Federal Trade Commission (FTC)
9015 Junction Drive
Annapolis Junction, MD20701
(877) 382-4357   www.ftc.gov

This brochure provides information about purchasing hearing aids, including information about federal standards and how to file a complaint. Free

Students Who are Deaf or Hard of Hearing in Postsecondary Education
HEATH Resource Center
George Washington University
2121 K Street, NW, Suite 220
Washington, DC 20037
(800) 544-3284 (V/TTY)   (202) 973-0904 (V/TTY)
FAX (202) 973-0908   askheath@heath.gwu.edu   www.heath.gwu.edu

This publication discusses the types of support services available, financial assistance, information for faculty and staff, and helpful publications. Free. Also available on the web site.

Tips for Communicating with Deaf and Hard-of-Hearing People
National Technical Institute for the Deaf (NTID)
Rochester Institute of Technology
Lyndon Baines Johnson Building
52 Lomb Memorial Drive
Rochester, NY 14623
(716) 475-6824 (V/TTY)   FAX (716) 475-6500
ntidmc@rit.edu   www.ntuc.rit.edu

This booklet offers suggestions for communicating one-to-one, in a group, through an interpreter, at an interview, at work, in writing, and on the telephone. Includes glossary of terms. $.35

Tips for Communicating with Hard of Hearing People
Self Help for Hard of Hearing People (SHHH)
7910 Woodmont Avenue, Suite 1200
Bethesda, MD 20814
(301) 657-2248   (301) 657-2249 (TTY)   FAX (301) 913-9413
webteam@hearingloss.org   www.hearingloss.org

These pocket guides provide helpful information to facilitate communication with individuals who are deaf. Available in English and Spanish. Available in sets of 10 cards, $2.75.

Using a TTY
United States Access Board
1331 F Street, NW, Suite 1000
Washington, DC 20004-1111
(800) 872-2253   (800) 993-2822 (TTY)   (202) 272-5434
(202) 272-5449 (TTY)   FAX (202) 272-5447
info@access-board.gov   www.access-board.gov

A brochure with basic information about TTYs (also called text telephones and teletypewriters). Free. Also available on the web site. The Access Board offers technical assistance on TTYs.

Working with Deaf People: Accessibility and Accommodation in the Workplace
by Susan B. Foster
Charles C. Thomas Publisher
2600 South First Street
Springfield, IL 62794
(800) 258-8980   (217) 789-8980   FAX (217) 789-9130
books@ccthomas.com   www.ccthomas.com

This book describes work adjustment problems from the perspectives of employers and individuals who are deaf and recommends strategies to solve them. $42.95;

VENDORS OF ASSISTIVE DEVICES

Listed below are manufacturers of assistive devices and mail order catalogues that specialize in devices for people who are deaf or have a hearing or speech impairment. Unless otherwise noted, catalogues include a variety of products and are free.

Artic Technologies
1000 John R Road, Suite 108
Troy, MI 48083
(248) 588-7370   FAX (248) 588-2650
info@artictech.com   www.artictech.com

Produces speech synthesis and screen access systems including hardware, software, voice tutorials, and accessories.

Automobility
DaimlerChrysler Corporation
PO Box 5080
Troy, MI 48007-5080
(800) 255-9877   (800) 922-3826 (TTY)
FAX (810) 597-3501   www.automobility.daimlerchrysler.com

Provides reimbursement (on eligible models) on the purchase of alerting devices for people who are deaf or hearing impaired and assistive equipment for vehicles purchased to transport individuals who use wheelchairs.

Clarity Products
4289 Bonny Oaks Drive, Suite 106
Chattanooga, TN 37406
(800) 552-3368   (800) 772-2889 (TTY)   (423) 622-7793
FAX (800) 325-8871   www.clarityproducts.com

Produces assistive telephone equipment such as amplified telephones and TTYs, alerting systems, and television caption decoders.

Communication Aids for Children and Adults
Crestwood Company
6625 North Sidney Place
Milwaukee WI 53209
(414) 352-5678   FAX (414) 352-5679
crestcomm@aol.com   www.communicationaids.com

Mail order catalogue with a wide variety of switches and other products for people who have both speech and mobility impairments.

Consultants for Communication Technology
508 Bellevue Terrace
Pittsburgh, PA 15202
(412) 761-6062   FAX (412) 761-7336
cct@ConCommTech.com   www.ConCommTech.com

Produces assistive technology for individuals with speech and mobility impairments including KeyWi2, software that enables a laptop computer to become a communication device without an external speech synthesizer. Environmental Control System is used to control TV, VCR, and lights using a PC or single switch. Phone Manager allows automatic telephone dialing and answering. Free demos available on web site and on disk.

Don Johnston, Inc.
26799 West Commerce Drive
Volo, IL 60073
(800) 999-4660   (847) 740-0749   FAX (847) 740-7326
info@donjohnston.com   www.donjohnston.com

Mail order catalogue of speech synthesizers used in conjunction with software programs that teach speech; adapted computer equipment; and publications.

Ford Mobility Motoring Program
PO Box 529
Bloomfield hills, MI 48303
(800) 952-2248   (800) 833-0312 (TTY)
FAX (248) 333-0300   mobilitymotoring@fordprogramhq.com
www.mobilitymotoringprogram.com

This program funds alerting systems for people with hearing impairments and assistive equipment for customers with mobility impairments.

General Motors Mobility Assistance Center
100 Renaissance Center, PO Box 100
Detroit, MI 48265
(800) 323-9935   (800) 833-9935 (TTY)
www.gm.com/automotive/vehicle_shopping/gm_mobility

This program provides reimbursements for modifications or assistive driving devices for new or demo vehicles. Includes alerting devices for drivers who are deaf or hearing impaired, such as emergency vehicle siren detectors and enhanced turn signal reminders.

GW Micro
725 Airport North Office Park
Fort Wayne, IN 46825
(260) 489-3671   FAX (260) 489-2608
support@gwmicro.com   www.gwmicro.com

Sells speech synthesizers, screen readers, and speech recognition software for PCs. Large print, audiocassette, and disk instruction manuals available. Also sells other vendors' computer systems, synthesizers, software, and accessories. Newsletter, "Voice of Vision," available on the web site. Free

Harris Communications
15155 Technology Drive
Eden Prairie, MN 55344
(800) 825-6758   (800) 825-9187 (TTY)   FAX (952) 906-1099
www.harriscomm.com

Distributes a wide variety of aids that enhance hearing, such as TTYs, assistive listening devices, alerting systems, and publications and tapes. Free catalogue.

Mobility by Volvo Center
PO Box 529
Bloomfield hills, MI 48303
(800) 803-5222   (800) 833-0312 (TTY)
FAX (248) 333-0300   mobilitybyvolvo@volvoprogramhq.com
www.volvocars.us/mobility

This program funds alerting systems for people with hearing impairments and assistive equipment for customers with mobility impairments and.

Oval Window Audio
33 Wildflower Court
Nederland, CO 80466
(303) 447-3607 (V/TT/FAX)   info@ovalwindowaudio.com
www.ovalwindowaudio.com

Produces induction assistive listening devices.

Phonic Ear
3880 Cypress Drive
Petaluma, CA 94954
(800) 227-0735   (707) 769-1110   FAX (707) 769-9624
customerservice@phonicear.com   www.phonic.ear.com

142

Produces the Easy Listener, a personal FM amplification system and other personal amplification systems.

Prentke Romich Company
1022 Heyl Road
Wooster, OH 44691
(800) 262-1984   (330) 262-1984   FAX (330) 263-4829
info@prentrom.com   www.prentrom.com

Produces augmentative communication systems and alternative computer access devices, including a variety of switches, special no-touch keyboards, and disk guides. Provides training in the use of their products.

Pulse Data HumanWare, Inc.
175 Mason Circle
Concord, CA 94520
(800) 722-3393   (925) 680-7100   FAX (925) 681-4630
usa@pulsedata.com   www.pulsedata.com

Produces and sells speech synthesizers, scanners, and software.

Williams Sound Corporation
10399 West 70th Street
Eden Prairie, MN 55344
(800) 328-6190   FAX (612) 943-2174
www.williamsound.com

Sells assistive listening devices for personal use and assistive listening systems for group listening.

Words+
1220 West Avenue J
Lancaster, CA 93534-2902
(800) 869-8521   (661) 723-6593   FAX (661) 723-2114
www.words-plus.com

Manufactures augmentative communication systems including hardware, software, and hand-held communications devices.

Chapter 9

MOBILITY IMPAIRMENTS

Mobility impairments may be caused by diseases or injuries and result in different types and degrees of disabilities. Cerebral palsy, multiple sclerosis, arthritis, spina bifida, and stroke are examples of diseases that may cause mobility impairments. Some individuals who contracted polio in the 1940s and 1950s are experiencing post-polio symptoms which include muscle weakness and fatigue. Injuries experienced as a result of accidents may result in either temporary or permanent mobility impairments. Low back pain, for example, is a common result of injury at the workplace. Spinal cord injuries, which are most commonly caused by accidents, usually result in paralysis with either all limbs paralyzed (quadriplegia) or paralysis of the legs (paraplegia). Amputations are sometimes necessitated by diabetes, circulatory diseases, or cancer.

Carpal tunnel syndrome results from pressure on the median nerve which passes through the wrist or carpal tunnel along with nine tendons. When the tendons are enlarged due to intensive repetitive movement, they put pressure on the median nerve, resulting in tingling or numbness, pain, or decreased sensitivity in the fingers.

Each case of mobility impairment is different. Some individuals may experience pain when they try to use their hands to operate a keyboard. Those individuals with the most severe mobility impairments may be unable to move any part of their body below the head. Technological advances in the development of assistive devices have enabled individuals with severe disabilities to operate wheelchairs, operate their own computers, and to control their environments.

Employment of workers who have mobility impairments is facilitated when employers are aware of the physical aspects of the environment that ensure a safe workplace and when they are knowledgeable about the many assistive devices available. Training members of the personnel or human resources department, supervisors, and co-workers about the needs of employees with mobility impairments improves working relations for all concerned.

Prior to assigning an employee with a mobility impairment to a particular position, a job analysis should be carried out to determine the specific requirements of each task assigned to the position. After determining the requirements of the job, the prospective employee's abilities should be examined along with the available assistive devices that can enable the employee to carry out the tasks. Do not assume that individuals who use wheelchairs are unable to stand or to perform physical activities. Many people who are able to walk, albeit with difficulty, use wheelchairs to conserve energy. Some individuals with paraplegia have developed strength in their upper extremities and may be able to perform physical tasks with the use of special wheelchairs that permit the user to stand up. Consultation with a rehabilitation engineer may be warranted. An existing device may be modified for a specific employee, a new one may be developed, or a simple modification of the environment may enable the employee to perform the job. Another option is to perform certain tasks jointly with an assistant or colleague. For example, carrying out a laboratory experiment with a colleague not only enables an employee with a mobility impairment to be more productive, but also encourages discussion of the procedures and results.

In 2003, the Food and Drug Administration (FDA) approved a battery-powered wheelchair that can climb stairs and curbs, elevate the user by becoming a two wheel chair, and traversing rough terrains. The "Independence iBOT enables the user to reach for objects at high levees and to hold a conversation at eye level with others. In order to use this chair, the individual must have the use of at least one hand in order to manipulate the button that controls the commands for the wheelchair to operate in different ways.

Farmers and agricultural workers who experience disability are reaping the benefits of technology as well as individuals with mobility impairments who live and work in urban settings. Programs funded through partnerships of federal, state, and private entities are providing education and technical assistance to rural and farm families.

Many organizations that provide direct services to people with mobility impairments have developed programs to help people with disabilities obtain or maintain employment. Both public and private service agencies can help current employees who have developed mobility impairments; they can also help employers recruit new employees. Employees may also benefit from a referral to these organizations in order to make sure that their assistive devices are up-to-date; to join self-help groups; or to obtain other services.

Vocational rehabilitation services are available to employees with chronic conditions that cause disabilities if they plan to continue working or to return to gainful employment. Vocational counseling, job evaluation, job modification, and training or retraining may be offered. Vocational rehabilitation services may pay for corrective devices such as splints and braces, medical or surgical treatment, and provision of assistive technology.

ASSISTIVE DEVICES AND ENVIRONMENTAL ADAPTATIONS

The number of assistive devices on the market has increased rapidly in recent years. While many of these products are a result of the rapid advances in computer technology, many other devices are neither high tech nor expensive. Some products designed for the general public are used by people with mobility impairments to help them function in their daily activities. Sometimes carpenters, engineers, or the individuals with disabilities themselves are able to adapt a product, design a product, or modify the work site simply and inexpensively.

Employers should consult with experts in the field of barrier-free design to ensure that their facilities enable employees with mobility impairments to enter and exit the building easily and safely; that bathroom facilities, water fountains, and employee dining rooms are accessible; that aisles and entryways are wide enough to accommodate wheelchairs, scooters, and walkers; and that ramps are placed where needed. Special paint or grit strip paint applied to slippery surfaces or inclines reduces the risk of accidents for people who use wheelchairs, walkers, scooters, or canes. Mirrors mounted at hallway intersections and see-through panels in doors may help prevent accidents for employees traveling in wheelchairs. Laboratory equipment and other furniture should be lowered to a height that is accessible to employees who use wheelchairs. Elevator buttons, public telephones, and light switches should also be accessible to people who use wheelchairs. Staff members who are not disabled should be assigned the responsibility for helping employees with mobility impairments to exit the building in case of an emergency, such as a fire, bomb threat, or toxic leak.

Transportation has often been a barrier to employment for individuals whose mobility impairments require them to use wheelchairs or walkers. Some employees with mobility impairments may be able to operate their own automobiles or vans. Many car manufacturers offer specially adapted vans to carry wheelchairs. Some of these companies also have special purchase or loan programs for people with disabilities for the purpose of transporting individuals who use wheelchairs. General Motors, Ford, Volvo, and DaimlerChrysler offer financial assistance for the purchase of assistive equipment such as hand controls, a ramp, or lifts to be installed in their vehicles (see "VENDORS OF ASSISTIVE DEVICES" section below). Public transportation systems may have regular buses with special equipment to lift wheelchairs, or they may offer transportation in specially designed vehicles for people with disabilities. Organizations that employ large numbers of people with mobility impairments may find that it is advantageous to lease transportation services or to operate their own van. Employees could each pay their share, just as they would if they took a bus or train to work, in order to cover the cost of the vehicle, maintenance, and the driver's salary. No matter what mode of transportation employees use, the entry from the parking lot should provide enough space for wheelchairs to be removed from the vehicle. Level ground or ramps should lead into the building. Special parking spaces should be designated for people with disabilities, and their use by other employees should be strictly prohibited.

The employee's work space should be examined to ensure that equipment and furniture are accessible. For employees who use wheelchairs, the space underneath the desk must be large enough to accommodate the wheelchair; file cabinets should be lateral so that employees can reach them. Special desks and workstations are available to accommodate wheelchairs and adjust to the required height of the user. Rectangular, L-shaped, or wrap-around work surfaces offer flexibility for employees with differing abilities. Where carpets are used, they should be low level pile to allow for easier mobility of wheelchairs. Elevators should be large enough to accommodate wheelchairs. Some individuals use standing wheelchairs that offer flexibility in adapting to the workplace as well as improving circulation, reducing pressure sores, and allowing users who are unable to stand on their own to make direct eye contact with colleagues without looking up from a seated position.

People with mobility impairments in their upper extremities are often unable to turn pages or to use traditional keyboards. Automatic page turners and alternatives to keyboards enable these individuals to read and write. Using a mouse with a keyboard may be easier for people with arthritis in their wrists, hands, or fingers. Hand, wrist, or forearm rests used with computer keyboards reduce fatigue and cumulative stress injuries. Miniature keyboards are also available for people who have limited range of motion in their upper extremities. Spring-loaded, self-opening scissors and cutting tools, automatic staplers and hole punches, and tools such as pliers reduce stress on finger and hand joints. Doorknobs should be replaced with levers or outfitted with ridged plastic covers that provide an easy grip.

Rotary card files systems are available in carousel or motorized models. A wide variety of reaching tools, equipped with lever or trigger grips and magnetic or suction cup tips, enable employees who cannot easily bend or reach to retrieve small items. Keyguards fit over a computer keyboard enabling users to slide their hands across the keyboard without erroneously pressing unwanted keys. When the desired key is reached, the user presses it through the keyguard hole. Disk guards provide alignment with the disk drive opening and stability for employees with poor hand control. The disk rests on the guard and is easier to slide into the drive.

In some cases, devices designed for the general public may prove useful to individuals with limited hand strength. For example, the use of a speaker phone with automatic dialing or a headset instead of a telephone handset enables individuals with limited hand strength to make telephone calls easily. Automatic dialers allow users to enter telephone numbers into memory via a keypad, then dial them by pressing a button on the unit or holding the dialer to the receiver. Telephones that recognize voice patterns enable users to program frequently used numbers into the phone and recall them for dialing by using a voice command. Foam hair rollers, water pipe foam insulation, or layers of tape may be used to build up the handles of items as varied as pens, pencils, paint brushes, and other devices with handles to make gripping easier. For individuals who have experienced injuries from repetitive motion, adapted tools and changes in the height of the work surface may prove useful.

People who have low back pain often work in occupations that require lifting and bending. Automated lifting and hoisting devices can facilitate the work for these employees. Furniture that is designed to take the stress off the affected area of the back may also be useful. Proper seating is important for people with low back pain as well as for people who use wheelchairs. Many office chairs have been specially designed to reduce stress from the lower back. A foot rest relieves pressure on the back. Wheelchairs also come in many different types of models. If an employee who uses a wheelchair is experiencing pressure sores or discomfort, a change in his or her wheelchair may be warranted.

Work hardening programs are commonly used for employees who have experienced back injuries; they are also useful for people with arthritis and other musculoskeletal disorders. Work hardening is a term used to describe a plan developed specifically for an individual employee's needs. The first step in a work hardening program is to assess the employee's physical abilities and impairments; the use of medications; and psychological responses to the disability. Using the information obtained from this assessment, a program is designed to gradually build up the employee's strengths to cope with the requirements of the job. Employees learn safe, efficient ways of performing the required tasks. Work hardening programs are usually developed and supervised by occupational or physical therapists. The Commission on Accreditation of Rehabilitation Facilities (CARF) has established standards for work hardening programs (Doherty: 1990; Peters: 1990).

The variety of devices available to assist individuals with mobility impairments has grown rapidly as a result of the increased use of personal computer technology. People with minimal mobility can control their environment through the use of switches, headpointers, joysticks, and sip-and-puff switches; these devices are used in conjunction with special software or adapted hardware. For example, people with high quadriplegia are able to turn electrical devices on and off through the use of a sip-and-puff device. Switches that may be operated by a toe, a foot, or a hand enable individuals to enter data into computers. Headpointers are attached to a headset and consist of pointers with rubber tips that are used to control keys on the keyboard. Joysticks enable people with limited motion to simulate the movement of a mouse.

Individuals whose conditions limit their mobility and prevent them from speaking may carry out conversations by using switches in combination with speech synthesizers. (see Chapter 8, "Hearing and Speech Impairments" for vendors of speech synthesizers). Some devices are able to input information into computers by tracking the eyegaze of the user. The user selects the character or word that he or she wishes to use by fixing his or her gaze upon it. This process may be very time consuming, as it is usually necessary to scan a list of words and choose the one required. In order to increase the speed of scanning, methods of abbreviating and using Morse code have been developed.

Speech recognition systems enable individuals who are severely limited in their mobility to use personal computers in a variety of situations. These systems recognize the user's voice as an alternative way of entering data into computers. Individuals may use these systems to write and to carry out conversations, both on the job and in other settings.

Robots to carry out everyday tasks offer the hope that individuals with severe disabilities will be able to regain functional independence by issuing simple verbal commands. Some robots are already available, often carrying out assembly line tasks, while research to develop more advanced robots is ongoing. Undoubtedly, these devices will open a new world of employment to individuals who are severely disabled.

Case Vignette

Ken Foster, Returning to Farming with Spinal Cord Injury

Ken Foster sustained injuries that resulted in paralysis in his lower limbs (paraplegia) as the result of an automobile accident. After initial treatment in a local hospital emergency room, he was transferred to an acute care hospital in a nearby metropolitan area and then to a spinal cord injury center.

Ken had dreamed of taking over his family's farm as his father neared retirement. His education had prepared him to use modern business techniques in managing the farm, but how would he handle the physical requirements? He felt that his dream was shattered due to the paralysis. Farming had changed drastically since his boyhood days. How could he use the farm machinery? Could he afford to hire workers to assist him? What else could he do?

When he expressed these fears to Barry Nevins, the social worker at the spinal cord injury center, Barry suggested that he speak with a representative of the Farm Life and Rural Rehabilitation Association. Since 1988 the association had been assisting rural and farm families to continue farming as a way of life.

Ken agreed to meet with staff member Jed Reynolds and the occupational and physical therapists who had worked with him at the spinal cord injury center. Jed described the vocational, agricultural worksite assessment, and independent living services available through the program. Occupational therapist Nancy Sullivan and physical therapist Joan Landis described Ken's rehabilitation progress and his level of functioning. Since Ken was to be discharged from the spinal cord injury center in several weeks, they decided to visit Ken's farm to evaluate his accessibility needs and to help him overcome the obstacles to his future as a farmer.

Jed asked Ken if he would like to talk with several other farmers with disabilities in the area who were farming successfully. An informal peer support network had developed as the association identified farm families in need of support services and adaptive technology. Despite initial misgivings, Ken agreed to talk with Jim Barnes, who was farming in a nearby county. Jim, too, had sustained an injury which had caused paralysis in his lower limbs.

Continued on next page

149

As Jim described the techniques he used to accomplish everyday farm duties, Ken began to feel that all was not lost. Jim had suggestions for many of the problems Ken related. Jim used a hydraulic lift to move from his wheelchair to the tractor cab and harvesting equipment. An automatic hitching device allowed him to hitch and unhitch equipment from a seated position. He used a mobile cellular telephone when out in the field to stay in touch with family members and to contact them in case of emergency. His neighbors had helped to build and install several ramps to make farm buildings accessible. Jim was enthusiastic about the assistance he had received from others in the peer technology support group. Many of them had used stock materials to create their own assistive devices. Jim also confided that his wife and children were much more understanding of his disability and abilities after they visited with his new friends' families.

Barry Nevins referred Ken's case to the state division of vocational rehabilitation. The agricultural worksite assessment made by Jed Reynolds alerted the vocational counselor to Ken's needs. Since the assessment included possible solutions, a list of vendors of assistive devices, and estimated costs for accommodations, Ken's individualized written rehabilitation program (IWRP) was developed smoothly. The state vocational rehabilitation services would pay for some of the suggested modifications; Ken's health and disability insurance would fund others that were deemed medically necessary as well as useful in performing work.

Ken decided to use the computer skills he had learned in college to manage the farm accounts. Although he had no difficulty in using a conventional computer system, he asked for assistance in renovating a room to create accessible office space. A wall-mounted desk provided the room he needed for access in his wheelchair. File cabinets with side access, wall-mounted bookcases, and electrical outlets mounted within easy reach provided additional independence.

Ken and his family have discussed the role reversals that may prove necessary to accomplish tasks that technology cannot. His wife and children help with the lighter farm duties while he operates the heavy machinery. Occasionally he asks his son to check the grain bin level since he cannot climb up to do so. His wife is considering looking for a part-time job in town to supplement the family's income while Ken adjusts to farming with a disability. He and his family are looking forward to getting on with their lives and feel capable of solving other problems as they arise.

SUGGESTIONS FOR A SAFE AND FRIENDLY WORKPLACE

The following suggestions will help co-workers get along with employees with mobility impairments and make the environment a safe place for all:

- Make certain that aisles and hallways are wide enough to accommodate wheelchairs, electric scooters, and walkers and that they are free of clutter and protruding objects.

- When you see colleagues who have a mobility impairment in a difficult situation, ask if they need assistance. Just as anyone else would, they will tell you if they can handle the situation themselves or if they would like some help. Do not be offended if they reply that they do not need assistance. Examples of such situations include offering to reach for an item or to carry a heavy item for someone who has limited strength or mobility in the upper extremities. Offer a chair if the individual will have to remain standing for a long time. In some settings, a person who uses a wheelchair will need some assistance in getting past a barrier. Hold the door open for a person who uses a wheelchair or walker.

- Extend your hand for a handshake, but let the person with limited mobility or hand strength determine the grip, if any.

- When arranging for a group meeting of employees, be certain that the physical setting accommodates wheelchairs comfortably, so that wheelchair users feel that they fit in, both literally and figuratively. Taking the small amount of extra effort to do this gives wheelchair users a sense of belonging.

- When speaking to individuals who are seated in wheelchairs or scooters, be certain to look at them, not above them. Sit down beside the individual so that you are at eye level.

- When giving directions to a person who uses a wheelchair or scooter, be certain that the route is accessible.

- When walking with a person who has a mobility impairment, move at the same pace as that person and do not be impatient.

- When telephoning individuals with mobility impairments, be sure to let the phone ring longer than usual in order to give them time to reach the telephone.

References

Doherty, Connie
1990   "Beyond Work Hardening 101" <u>Work</u> Fall: 62-68
Peters, Pamela
1990   "Successful Return to Work Following A Musculoskeletal Injury" <u>American Association of Occupational Health Nurses Journal</u> 38 (June):6:264-27

ORGANIZATIONS

American Back Society (ABS)
St. Joseph's Professional Center
2647 International Boulevard, Suite 401
Oakland, CA 94601
(510) 536-9929   FAX (510) 536-1812
info@ambericanbacksoc.org   www.americanbacksoc.org

A membership organization dedicated to relieving the pain and impairment caused by back problems. Sponsors symposia for presenting research findings. Membership for licensed health care professionals, $225.00; for other interested individuals, $125.00. Publishes quarterly "ABS Newsletter," which is a benefit of membership, or it may be purchased for $62.50 a year.

American Chronic Pain Association (ACPA)
PO Box 850
Rocklin, CA 95677
(800) 533-3231   FAX (916) 632-3208
ACPA@pacbell.net   www.theacpa.org

Organizes groups to provide support and activities for people who experience chronic pain. Membership, $30.00 for new members includes "The Patient to Person: First Steps;" renewals, $15.00; includes quarterly newsletter, "ACPA Chronicle."

American Pain Society (APS)
4700 West Lake Avenue
Glen View, IL 60025
(847) 375-4715   FAX (877) 734-8758
info@ampainsoc.org   www.ampainsoc.org

A multidisciplinary membership organization that has the goals of advancing research, education, and professional services for people in pain. Membership dues for professionals vary by income level starting at $120.00. Individual membership, $150.00. Membership includes the quarterly publication "Pain Forum" and a newsletter, the "APS Bulletin."

Arthritis Foundation
PO Box 7669
Atlanta, GA 30357-0669
(800) 283-7800   (404) 872-7100
FAX (404) 872-0457   www.arthritis.org

Supports research; offers referrals to physicians; provides public and professional education. Chapters throughout the U.S.; toll-free number connects to local chapter. Some chapters offer arthritis classes, clubs, and exercise programs. Membership, $20.00, includes the Arthritis Foundation's "Drug Guide," chapter newsletter, and magazine, "Arthritis Today." Also available by subscription, $12.95. Members receive discounts on purchases of publications. Many brochures are available on the web site. Several brochures are available in Spanish.

Breaking New Ground Resource Center and Outreach Center
Purdue University
1146 ABE Building
West Lafayette, IN 47907-1146
(800) 825-4264   (765) 494-5088 (V/TTY)   FAX (765) 496-1356
www.breakingnewground.info   ·

A federally funded research center that investigates ways to improve opportunities for employment of farmers with disabilities. Provides assistive technology and outreach.Newsletter, "Breaking New Ground," available in standard print and on audiocassette. Free

Christopher and Dana Reeve Resource Center
Short Hills Plaza
636 Morris Turnpike, Suite 3A
Short Hills, NJ 07078
(800) 539-7309   info@paralysis.org   www.paralysis.org

Part of the Christopher Reeve Paralysis Foundation (see below), this federally funded center provides information on spinal cord injury to individuals and their caregivers. Publishes "Paralysis Resource Guide," free.

Christopher Reeve Paralysis Foundation
500 Morris Avenue
Springfield, NJ 07081
(800) 225-0292   (973) 379-2690   FAX (973) 912-9433
info@crpf.org   www.crpf.org

Supports research to find a cure for paralysis caused by spinal cord injury and other central nervous system disorders. Publishes "Walking Tomorrow," a newsletter about the organization's activities, and "Progress in Research," a newsletter about spinal cord injury research. Free. Also available on the web site. Various levels of membership fees.

Commission on Accreditation of Rehabilitation Facilities (CARF)
4891 East Grant Road
Tucson, AZ 85712
(888) 281-6531(V/TTY)   (520) 325-1044   FAX (520) 318-1129   www.carf.org

Conducts site evaluations and accredits organizations that provide rehabilitation. Established standards for work hardening rehabilitation programs. Web site has searchable database for providers that are accredited by CARF.

National AgrAbility Project
University of Wisconsin - Extension
Biological Systems Engineering Department
460 Henry Mall
Madison, WI 53706
(866) 259-6280   FAX (608) 262-0613
rschuler@facstaff.wisc.edu   www.agrabilityproject.org

Provides training, technical assistance, and information to state agrability projects. State agrability projects provide training and technical assistance directly to farmers with disabilities.

National Chronic Pain Outreach Association (NCPOA)
7979 Old Georgetown Road, Suite 100
Bethesda, MD 20814
(301) 652-4948   FAX (301) 907-0745
neurosurgery.mgh.harvard.edu/ncpainoa.htm

A national clearinghouse for information about chronic pain. Refers individuals to health care professionals and support groups on chronic pain throughout the U.S. Produces publications and audiocassettes on a variety of topics related to chronic pain. Membership, individuals, $25.00; professionals, $50.00; includes quarterly newsletter, "Lifeline."

National Easter Seals Society
230 West Monroe Street, Suite 1800
Chicago, IL 60606-4802
(800) 221-6827   (312) 726-6200   (312) 726-4258 (TTY)
FAX (312) 726-1494   info@easter-seals.org
www.easter-seals.org

Promotes research, education, and rehabilitation for people with physical disabilities.

National Multiple Sclerosis Society
733 Third Avenue
New York, NY 10017-3288
(212) 986-3240   FAX (212) 986-7981
(800) 344-4867 Information Resource Center and Library
Nat@nationalmssociety.org   www.nationalmssociety.org

Provides professional and public education and information and referral; supports research. Offers counseling services, physician referrals, advocacy, discount prescription and health care products program, and assistance in obtaining assistive equipment. Regional affiliates throughout the U.S. Information Resource Center and Library answers telephone inquiries from 11:00 a.m. to 5:00 p.m. E.S.T., Monday through Thursday. Membership, $25.00, includes large print magazine, "Inside MS," published three times a year. Newsletter also available on the web site. Individuals with multiple sclerosis may receive a courtesy membership if they are unable to pay.

National Spinal Cord Injury Association (NSCIA)
6701 Democracy Boulevard, Suite 300-9
Bethesda, MD 20817
(800) 962-9629   (301) 588-6959
FAX (301) 588-9414   nscia2@aol.com   www.spinalcord.org

A membership organization with chapters throughout the U.S. Disseminates information to people with spinal cord injuries and to their families; provides counseling; and advocates for the removal of barriers to independent living. Participates in the development of standards of care for regional spinal cord injury care. NSCIA will perform a customized database search; call for details. Holds annual meeting and educational seminars. Membership is free for individuals with a disability or family members and for professionals who provide services to individuals with spinal cord injuries. Monthly electronic newsletter, free.

Paralyzed Veterans of America (PVA)
801 18th Street, NW
Washington, DC 20006
(800) 424-8200   (800) 795-4327 (TTY)   (202) 416-7619
FAX (202) 785-4452   info@pva.org   www.pva.org

A membership organization for veterans with spinal cord injury. Advocates and lobbies for the rights of paralyzed veterans and sponsors research. Membership fees are set by state chapters. The national office refers callers to the nearest chapter. The PVA Spinal Cord Injury Education and Training Foundation accepts applications to fund continuing education, post-professional specialty training, and patient/client and family education. The PVA Spinal Cord Research Foundation accepts applications to fund basic and clinical research, the design of assistive devices, and conferences that foster interaction among scientists and health care providers. Some publications are available on the web site. Distributes an e-newsletter. Free

Rehabilitation Engineering and Assistive Technology Society of North America/RESNA
1700 North Moore Street, Suite 1540
Arlington, VA 22209
(703) 524-6686   (703) 524-6639 (TTY)   FAX (703) 524-6630
natloffice@resna.org   www.resna.org

Interdisciplinary membership organization for the advancement of rehabilitation and assistive technology. Special interest groups include wheeled mobility and seating, robotics, job accommodation, computer applications, and universal access. Professional specialty groups for manufacturers and suppliers of rehabilitation products, rehabilitation engineers, occupational therapists, and other professionals. Membership, $150.00, includes semi-annual journal, "Assistive Technology," and bimonthly "RESNA Newsletter." Subscription to "Assistive Technology" only, individuals, $65.00; institutions, $75.00

Rehabilitation Engineering and Research Center on Wheeled Mobility
Center for Assistive Technology and Environmental Accessibility (CATEA)
Georgia Institute of Technology
490 10th Street, NW
Atlanta, GA 30332-0156
(800) 726-9119   (404) 894-4960 (V/TTY)
FAX (404) 894-9320   www.mobilityrrerc.catea.org

This federally funded project conducts research to understand the needs of people who use wheelchairs and to develop products that meet those needs.

Trace Research and Development Center
University of Wisconsin-Madison
2107 Engineering Center Building
1550 Engineering Drive
Madison, WI 53706
(608) 262-6966   (608) 263-5408 (TTY)
FAX (608) 262-8848   info@trace.wisc.edu   trace.wisc.edu

Conducts research to make off-the-shelf technology more accessible to individuals with disabilities through universal design.

United Cerebral Palsy Association (UCPA)
1660 L Street, NW, Suite 700
Washington, DC 20036
(800) 872-5827   (202) 776-0406   (202) 973-7197
FAX (202) 776-0414   webmaster@ucpa.org   www.ucpa.org

Member groups throughout the country provide treatment, information, education, and counseling.

Vocational Rehabilitation Services
Veterans Benefits Administration
Department of Veterans Affairs (VA)
810 Vermont Avenue, NW
Washington, DC 20420
(202) 273-5400   (800) 827-1000 (connects with regional office)
FAX (202) 273-7485   www.va.gov

Provides education and rehabilitation assistance and independent living services to veterans with service related disabilities through offices located in every state as well as regional centers, medical centers, and insurance centers. Medical services are provided at VA Medical Centers, Outpatient Clinics, Domiciliaries, and Nursing Homes.

PUBLICATIONS AND TAPES

AGRICultural Online Access (AGRICOLA)
U.S. Department of Agriculture
National Agriculture Library, Reference Section
10301 Baltimore Boulevard, Room 300
Beltsville, MD 20705
(301) 504-5755   (301) 504-6856 (TTY)   agref@nal.usda.gov
www.nal.usda.gov

A bibliographic database that includes information for farming and homemaking for individuals with disabilities. Searches available on the web site. Charges for lending library posted on the web site.

ANSI/RESNA Wheelchair Standards
RESNA Press
1700 North Moore Street, Suite 1540
Arlington, VA 22209
(703) 524-6686   (703) 524-6639 (TTY)   FAX (703) 524-6630
natloffice@resna.org   www.resna.org

Developed jointly by RESNA and the American National Standards Institute (ANSI), these standards apply to manual and electric wheelchairs and scooters (Volume One) and electric wheelchairs and scooters only (Volume Two). Two volume set, $550.00; volume 1, $300.00; volume 2, $250.00.

Arthritis in the Workplace
Arthritis Foundation
PO Box 7669
Atlanta, GA 30357-0669
(800) 283-7800   (404) 872-7100
FAX (404) 872-0457   www.arthritis.org

This booklet discusses working successfully with arthritis and makes suggestions for disclosing this chronic condition, dealing with co-workers, joint protection, and workplace modifications. Single copy, free.

Back Pain
Info Vision
102 North Hazel Street
Glenwood, IA 51534
(800) 237-1808   FAX (888) 735-2622   iviowa@aol.com

This videotape discusses prevention of recurrent back pain and when exercise helps or hurts the condition. Includes medication choices and how to decide when surgery is required. 30 minutes. $20.00

The Back Pain Book
by Mike Hage
Peachtree Publishers
1700 Chattahoochee Avenue
Atlanta, GA 30318
(800) 241-0113   FAX (800) 875-8909   (404) 876-8761
FAX (404) 875-2578   www.peachtree-online.com

Written by a physical therapist, this book discusses how movement and posture may alleviate neck and back pain. $14.95

Carpal Tunnel Syndrome
Arthritis in the Workplace
Arthritis Foundation
PO Box 7669
Atlanta, GA 30357-0669
(800) 283-7800   (404) 872-7100
FAX (404) 872-0457   www.arthritis.org

This publication describes the causes, medications, and workplace changes to improve the condition. Free. Also available on the web site.

Farming with an Upper Extremity Amputation
Breaking New Ground Resource Center
Purdue University
1146 ABE Building
West Lafayette, IN 47907-1146
(800) 825-4264   (765) 494-5088 (V/TTY)   FAX (765) 496-1356
www.breakingnewground.info

This videotape discusses techniques used by farmers with arm amputations and shows machinery and tool adaptations. 23 minutes. $75.00

Low Back Pain Fact Sheet
National Institute of Neurological Disorders and Stroke (NINDS)
PO Box 5801
Bethesda, MD 20824
(800) 352-9424   FAX (301) 402-2186
braininfo@ninds.nh.gov   www.ninds.nih.gov

160

This publication describes the causes, diagnostic techniques, prevention, and treatment of low back pain. Free. Also available on the web site.

National Database of Educational Resources on Spinal Cord Injury
The Institute for Rehabilitation and Research (TIRR)
Division of Education, B 107
1333 Moursund
Houston, TX 77030
(800) 732-8124   FAX (713) 797-5982
hullt@tirr.tmc.edu   www.tirr.org

This database of publications, audiocassettes, and videotapes covers topics such as environmental modifications and accessibility, adaptive equipment and aids, vocational management, and recreation and leisure. Available online at www.MSCISDisseminationCenter.org. Entries that are specific to women or men are marked. Includes section on "Sexuality, Marriage, Pregnancy, and Fertility." For those without Internet access, TIRR will take phone requests for two searches at no charge.

PN/Paraplegia News
2111 East Highland Avenue, Suite 180
Phoenix, AZ 85016
(888) 888-2201   (602) 224-0500   FAX (602) 224-0507
info@pnnews.com   www.pn-magazine.com

A monthly magazine sponsored by the Paralyzed Veterans of America. Features information for paralyzed veterans and civilians, articles about everyday living, new legislation, employment, and research. $23.00

Resources for People with Disabilities and Chronic Conditions
Resources for Rehabilitation
22 Bonad Road
Winchester, Massachusetts 01890
(781) 368-9094   FAX (781) 368-9096   info@rfr.org
www.rfr.org

A comprehensive resource guide with chapters on spinal cord injuries, low back pain, diabetes, multiple sclerosis, Parkinson's disease, hearing and speech impairments, vision impairment and blindness, and epilepsy. Includes information about the disease or condition; psychological aspects of the condition; environmental adaptations; assistive technology; and descriptions of organizations, publications, and products. $56.95. (See order form on last page of this book.)

Say Goodbye to Back Pain
Video Learning Library
15838 North 62nd Street
Scottsdale, AZ 85254
(800) 383-8811   (480) 596-9970   FAX (480) 596-9973
jspencer@videolearning. com   www.videomarketplace.com

This videotape describes a six week exercise program for individuals with back pain. 96 minutes. Available on videotape with accompanying booklet, $39.95

Specifications for Making Buildings and Facilities Accessible to, and Usable by, Physically Handicapped People
Global Engineering
15 Inverness East
Glenwood, CO 80112
(800) 854-7179   FAX (314) 726-6418   www.global.ihs.com

Lists ANSI standards for barrier-free design. Order A117.1 - 1998. May be downloaded for web site, $26.00; print copy, $26.00

Spinal Network
by Barry Corbet et al. (eds.)
No Limits Communications
PO Box 220
Horsham, PA 19044
(888) 850-0344   (215) 675-9133   FAX (215) 675-9376
kim@leonardmedia.com   www.newmobility.com

This book describes the medical aspects of spinal cord injury and the wide variety of effects on functioning. Presents biographical accounts of people who have lived with spinal cord injuries. Discusses issues of everyday living, including sex, relationships, and parenting, recreation and sports, travel, and legal and financial concerns. $39.95

Voice Recognition Technology
PACER Center (Parent Advocacy Coalition for Educational Rights)
8161 Normandale Boulevard
Minneapolis, MN 55437
(888) 248-0822   (952) 838-9000
In MN, (800) 537-2237   (952) 838-0190 (TTY)
FAX (952) 838-0199   pacer@pacer.org   www.pacer.org

This publication discusses how voice recognition can help people with disabilities. It discusses the latest technology and provides a list of vendors and web sites. $3.00

<u>Work Hardening: State of the Art</u>
by Linda Ogden-Niemeyer and Karen Jacobs
Slack, Thorofare, NJ

This book explains the philosophy and purpose of work hardening and presents work activities
and case studies of 20 actual programs. Out of print

VENDORS OF ASSISTIVE DEVICES

Listed below are manufacturers of assistive devices, mail order catalogues that specialize in devices for people with mobility impairments, and automobile manufacturers that provide financial assistance for the purchase of assistive equipment. Unless otherwise noted, catalogues include a variety of products and are free.

Automobility
DaimlerChrysler Corporation
PO Box 5080
Troy, MI 48007-5080
(800) 255-9877   (800) 922-3826 (TTY)
FAX (810) 597-3501   www.automobility.daimlerchrysler.com

Provides reimbursement (on eligible models) on the purchase of alerting devices for people who are deaf or hearing impaired and assistive equipment for vehicles purchased to transport individuals who use wheelchairs.

Communication Aids for Children and Adults
Crestwood Company
6625 North Sidney Place
Milwaukee WI 53209
(414) 352-5678   FAX (414) 352-5679
crestcomm@aol.com   www.communicationaids.com

Mail order catalogue with a wide variety of switches and other products for people who have both speech and mobility impairments.

Consultants for Communication Technology
508 Bellevue Terrace
Pittsburgh, PA 15202
(412) 761-6062   FAX (412) 761-7336
cct@ConCommTech.com   www.ConCommTech.com

Produces assistive technology for individuals with speech and mobility impairments including KeyWi2, software that enables a laptop computer to become a communication device without an external speech synthesizer; Environmental Control System used to control TV, VCR, and lights using a PC or single switch; and Phone Manager, which allows automatic telephone dialing and answering. Free demos available on web site and on disk.

Don Johnston, Inc.
26799 West Commerce Drive
Volo, IL 60073
(800) 999-4660   (847) 740-0749   FAX (847) 740-7326
info@donjohnston.com   www.donjohnston.com

Mail order catalogue of devices that enable individuals with disabilities to have alternative access to computer operations. Produces Ke:nx, which provides a variety of alternative modes to access the Macintosh computer or PCs with Windows, using switches and specially designed keyboards.

ErgoSource
PO Box 695
Wayzata, MN 55391
(952) 404-1969   FAX (952) 404-1058   info@ergosource.com
www.ergosource.com

A catalogue of products such as workstations, chairs, foot rests, and ergonomic tools that are designed to prevent disorders including low back pain and carpal tunnel syndrome.

Ford Mobility Motoring Program
PO Box 529
Bloomfield hills, MI 48303
(800) 952-2248   (800) 833-0312 (TTY)
FAX (248) 333-0300   mobilitymotoring@fordprogramhq.com
www.mobilitymotoringprogram.com

This program funds assistive equipment for customers with mobility impairments and alerting systems for people with hearing impairments.

General Motors Mobility Assistance Center
100 Renaissance Center, PO Box 100
Detroit, MI 48265
(800) 323-9935   (800) 833-9935 (TTY)
www.gm.com/automotive/vehicle_shopping/gm_mobility

This program provides reimbursements for modifications or assistive driving devices for new or demo vehicles. Includes alerting devices for drivers who are deaf or hearing impaired, such as emergency vehicle siren detectors and enhanced turn signal reminders.

IBM Accessibility Center
11400 Burnet Road
Austin, TX 78758
(800) 426-4832   www.ibm.com/able

Produces the Independence Series of accessible products that helps people with disabilities use personal computers. The WebSphere Voice Server enables the user to conduct e-business by accessing applications and data via telephone.

Independence iBOT
Independence Technology
877 794-3125   FAX (877) 794-3129
customerzone@indus.jnj.com   www.independencenow.com

Manufactures the iBOT Mobility System, a battery powered wheelchair that enables users to press a button to command the chair to stand on two legs for reaching or eye level conversations, to climb steps and curbs, and to travel on various types of terrain.

In Touch Systems
11 Westview Road
Spring Valley, NY 10977
(800) 332-6244   (914) 354-7431
sc@magicwandkeyboard.com   www.magicwandkeyboard.com

Manufactures the Magic Wand Keyboard, a miniature keyboard and mouse for PCs or Macintosh computers for individuals with restricted hand movement. Uses a hand-held wand or mouthstick to select keys.

Keytec
1293 North Plano Road
Richardson, TX 75081
(800) 624-4289   (972) 234-8617   FAX (972-234-8542
sales@magictouch.com   www.magictouch.com

Sells Magic Touch, a pressure sensitive overlay for computer screens, that allows individuals with restricted hand movements to touch the screen rather than use a mouse to control the cursor. Available for Windows or Macintosh. Prices vary depending on model.

LC Technologies
9455 Silver King Court
Fairfax, VA 22031
(800) 393-4293   (703) 385-7133
FAX (703) 385-7137   info0309@eyegaze.om   www.eyegaze.com

Manufactures the Eyegaze Computer System which enables individuals with severe mobility impairments to use their eyes to control devices in their environment, to use the telephone, and to use a computer. A 25 minute videotape demonstration of the Eyegaze Computer System is available, free.

Mobility by Volvo Center
PO Box 529
Bloomfield hills, MI 48303
(800) 803-5222   (800) 833-0312 (TTY)
FAX (248) 333-0300   mobilitybyvolvo@volvoprogramhq.com
www.volvocars.us/mobility

This program funds assistive equipment for customers with mobility impairments and alerting systems for people with hearing impairments.

Prentke Romich Company
1022 Heyl Road
Wooster, OH 44691
(800) 262-1984   (330) 262-1984   FAX (330) 263-4829
info@prentrom.com   www.prentrom.com

Produces augmentative communication systems and alternative computer access devices, including a variety of switches, special no-touch keyboards, and disk guides. Provides training in the use of their products.

Rolli-Moden Designs
12225 World Trade Drive, Suite T
San Diego, CA 92128
(800) 707-2395   (858) 676-1825   FAX (858) 676-0820
rm@roli-moden.com   www.rolli-moden.com

Sells dress and casual clothing and accessories designed for wheelchair users. Free catalogue.

ScanSoft Company
9 Centennial Drive
Peabody, MA 01960
(978) 977-2000   www.scansoft.com

Produces the Dragon NaturallySpeaking software system, which converts dictated speech into text in a Windows application.

Touch Turner
13621 103rd Avenue NE
Arlington, WA 98223
(888) 811-1962   (360) 651-1962
FAX (360) 658-9380   sales@touchturner.com   www.touchturner.com

Manufactures a product that turns pages of books, available with a variety of switches. Operates on batteries or with electrical adaptor.

Voice Connexion, Inc.
10522 Covington Circle
Villa Park, CA 92861
(714) 685-1066   FAX (714) 628-1321   voicecnx@aol.com
www.voicecnx.com

Manufactures voice recognition and speech synthesis hardware and software for PCs.

Chapter 10

VISUAL IMPAIRMENT AND BLINDNESS

One of the greatest fears of individuals who are visually impaired or blind is that they will be unable to obtain or retain employment. As of 1997, the majority of individuals who had problems seeing were not employed; only 41.5% were employed (McNeil: 2001). With advances in modern technology, however, people who are visually impaired or blind are capable of carrying out many job functions that would have been closed to them in the past. It is important that both employers and employees themselves be made aware of the many types of assistive equipment that can enable them to keep working in their current positions or enter new positions. Obviously, for those individuals who are engaged in careers which require excellent vision, such as airplane pilots, truck drivers, and certain medical specialists, retraining or additional education will be required to seek out new fields of endeavor.

Visual impairment will become an issue of increasing importance to employers as the workforce ages, since aging is strongly related to irreversible vision loss. Therefore, it is important that employers learn about the different types and degrees of visual impairment and their effects on performing specific job functions. This knowledge will correct erroneous stereotypes about individuals who are visually impaired or blind and enable employers to utilize the talents and skills of this group of workers to the maximum extent possible.

Most individuals who are visually impaired retain some useful vision. These individuals are often able to continue working with the help of magnifiers, telescopes attached to their glasses, or other optical aids. These optical aids enable them to continue reading and writing, sometimes using large print materials, and to continue manual tasks performed in factories and other settings. In addition, the rapid advances in computer technology have been a boon to workers who are visually impaired or blind.

Central vision loss and peripheral field loss are two major types of visual impairment. *Central vision* enables people to read and to recognize faces. Individuals use *peripheral vision* for mobility and to see the full scope of the scene they are facing. Diminished peripheral vision is often referred to as tunnel vision. This impairment affects mobility, although the central vision may still be intact. Thus, employees who have peripheral vision loss may be able to carry out job tasks that require acute vision for close work, such as reading or assembling small parts, but they may have trouble getting around the facility. Individuals with central vision loss may have problems with job tasks that require acute vision but may be able to get around the facility and carry out other tasks without any aids or assistance.

Some individuals have progressive diseases that may cause their vision to decrease as time passes. Examples of these diseases are retinitis pigmentosa and macular degeneration (see Living with Low Vision: A Resource Guide for People with Sight Loss for a description of these eye diseases; described in "PUBLICATIONS AND TAPES" section below). These individuals may need to have their work environment modified as their vision deteriorates. Sometimes increased light or magnification is sufficient to enable employees with visual impairments to perform their jobs; in other instances they may require equipment with large print or speech output.

Individuals who are totally blind or who have light perception only will require different types of adaptations than individuals who retain useful vision. These individuals will often use braille to read and write documents, although they use regular typewriters as well. Although sighted co-workers are probably unable to read and write braille, computers that are designed to be used with braille also transcribe the data into standard print output.

To obtain information about recruiting employees who are visually impaired or blind or to make the necessary adaptations for current employees, employers should contact the state vocational rehabilitation agency that serves individuals who are visually impaired or blind, a private rehabilitation counselor, or a private agency. In some states, there are two vocational rehabilitation agencies; one that serves individuals who are visually impaired or blind and another that serves individuals with other types of disabilities. In other states, one agency serves people with all types of disabilities, including vision impairment and blindness.

Many states require that individuals be legally blind in order to qualify for state services. In the United States, the definition of *legal blindness* is a visual acuity of 20/200 or worse in the better eye with all possible correction (glasses) or a visual field of 20 degrees diameter or less in the better eye. The classification of legal blindness entitles individuals to tax benefits and to rehabilitation services provided by state governments. *Low vision* is the term that is commonly used to refer to visual impairments that leave the individual with some residual vision. Although there are no standard definitions of low vision, professionals usually consider an acuity of 20/70 or worse in the better eye to be low vision.

Employees who are visually impaired but who are not legally blind should not wait for their eye disease or condition to progress to legal blindness before seeking vocational rehabilitation. Many types of accommodations can be made to help them retain their jobs, including assistive aids, changes in responsibilities and schedules, and trading responsibilities with other employees. These employees should contact private agencies or private rehabilitation professionals who assess visual functioning, the requirements of the position, and suggest available modifications and equipment that may help. In some instances, the vocational rehabilitation professional may suggest that the employee be transferred to another position or enroll in a training program to learn new skills.

The Department of Veterans Affairs has identified veterans who are legally blind as a special interest group that requires a coordinated approach to VA services and has established the VIST (Visual Impairment Services Team) Program. These veterans are eligible for counseling services and job assistance at Career Development Centers located in VA regional offices. These offices also offer a Vocational Rehabilitation and Counseling Service to help veterans with service-connected disabilities receive rehabilitation services and find employment. The local Veteran Employment Representatives and Disabled Veteran Outreach Programs also provide services to veterans who are visually impaired or blind. A booklet describing the benefits and rights of U.S. veterans, "Federal Benefits for Veterans and Dependents," is available from the web site of the Consumer Information Center: www.pueblo.gsa.gov.

ENVIRONMENTAL ADAPTATIONS

The work environment often may be made accessible for employees who are visually impaired or blind without great effort or expense. Simple modifications will result in less anxiety for people with vision loss, and co-workers will be less concerned about them falling or bumping into objects. Two obvious examples are providing good lighting and eliminating all possible sources of glare.

The work environment should have well-lighted hallways and accessible entries. Some people with vision loss also have other disabilities and may use walkers, canes, scooters, or wheelchairs for mobility. Corridors and aisles should be wide enough to accommodate these mobility aids and should be cleared of clutter and projecting objects. Drinking fountains and public telephones should be recessed. Elevators should have braille and raised numerals to indicate floors; taped announcements of the floor number are also helpful.

When designing or remodeling an office, the needs of employees who are visually impaired or blind should be a major concern. Contrasting colors should be used for carpeting, furniture, and walls. Placing yellow tape or painting stripes on the edge of steps helps people with visual impairment to navigate. A metal edge on a carpeted step or a change in the texture of the flooring will provide tactile cues for individuals who are blind. Doors should be kept either closed or completely open. Chairs should always be replaced under tables or desks. Partially-open doors and chairs left in the middle of a room are dangerous.

Personnel forms and office procedure manuals should be made available in large print, braille, disk, or on audiocassette. Signs should have large letters and good contrast. Telephones should be adapted with large print numerals for easy use by individuals who are visually impaired. Employees who are totally blind may find that raised dots on the 4-5-6 row of a telephone will guide them when dialing. A bold point pen used with bold line paper is a simple suggestion for carrying out everyday writing tasks. Writing guides, signature guides, and check writing guides help people to locate lines on a printed page or to line up their own handwritten lines.

SIGHTED GUIDE AND OTHER MOBILITY TECHNIQUES

All employees who work with individuals who are visually impaired or blind should be familiar with sighted guide technique (see Chapter 1, "Work and Disability" for information about educational programs for employers and co-workers). People with vision loss should never be pushed or pulled. These awkward methods cause anxiety and place the person with vision loss in an unsafe position. Not all people with vision loss need help with travel. Some people with central vision loss are able to move easily without any assistance as are some people with moderate peripheral vision loss. The first step, therefore, is to always ask the person whether he or she needs assistance.

If the person indicates that assistance is needed, the sighted person should offer the person who is visually impaired or blind his or her arm to hold just above the elbow and should walk a step ahead. By walking ahead of the person who is visually impaired or blind, the sighted guide provides information about the route ahead. For example, when the guide steps down a curb from the sidewalk to the street, the person with vision loss will feel that movement. When guiding the individual to a seat, place his or her hand on the back of the chair and indicate if it has arms or not. In addition, mentioning the approach to a flight of steps or the entry onto an escalator or elevator provides the person with vision loss with important information. When giving directions, never say "over here" or "over there." Use specific words such as "left" and "right." Even people who have adjusted to their vision loss and are comfortable getting around on their own will appreciate a sighted guide in unfamiliar settings.

A representative from a local private or public rehabilitation agency which serves individuals who are visually impaired or blind is usually able to provide a brief lesson in this technique. A request for training in sighted guide technique may also open the door to additional interactions with rehabilitation professionals.

Some individuals use a long white cane or guide dog to assist them with independent travel. The long white cane is swung in an arc in front of the user to detect objects ahead. Some white canes fold up for storage in a briefcase, pocketbook, or drawer. Individuals who are visually impaired or blind learn the special techniques of traveling independently with a long white cane from orientation and mobility (O & M) instructors. Some individuals do not use their canes all of the time; they may need them only in unfamiliar surroundings or in the dark.

Individuals who use guide dogs attend residential training programs or receive training in their own homes, where they learn to work with the dog in a variety of situations, such as urban settings, on public transportation, on escalators, and in rural areas. When the guide dog is harnessed, it is "working" and should never be petted or otherwise distracted. Guide dogs are trained to lead their owners safely around obstacles, to pause at steps and crosswalks, and to "willfully disobey" if commanded to go forward in an unsafe situation. Employers should expect the guide dog to be harnessed and kept near the employee, usually under a desk or beside a work station. The employee may request help in designating a grassy area or alternative to walk the dog once or twice during the day and may wish to have a bowl of water available for the dog. Guide dogs are generally assigned to individuals based on the master's temperament and vocation. German shepherds and retrievers are the most common breeds used as guide dogs. Co-workers should be knowledgeable about how to treat these specially trained dogs. Supervisors should be certain that co-workers in close proximity to a dog are not allergic to dogs or do not have fears or aversions to being near dogs.

ASSISTIVE DEVICES

Many people who are visually impaired or blind successfully gain employment or continue to work through the use of "high tech" electronic aids. These aids include closed circuit television systems (sometimes called video magnifiers) and computers with large print, speech, or braille output.

Closed circuit television systems are designed to magnify printed material electronically. The components are a mounted camera, a self-contained light source, a lens that magnifies print to various sizes or one size fixed to the individual's specifications, and a monitor. Monitors vary in size from 12 to 27 inches and are available in color and black and white. Some models may be used to magnify the screen output of computers.

172

The options for computer users who have experienced vision loss have increased dramatically over the past few years. Some popular computers on the market are equipped with features that enable users to magnify print size on the screen a specified number of times; for example, Macintosh computers include a standard feature called Close View. The Windows operating systems include a similar feature. A number of manufacturers produce browsers that facilitate use of the Internet for individuals who are visually impaired or blind.

Some software packages increase the size of print on the screen of PCs and Macintosh computers. In addition, large monitors, while usually more expensive than standard monitors, may enlarge print size and enable people with vision loss to continue using a standard computer.

Some individuals who are visually impaired or blind use synthetic speech screen access. Those with some useful vision often use speech in conjunction with magnification systems to reinforce what is displayed on the screen and reduce fatigue. This combination of magnification and speech often allows the use of less magnification, thereby increasing the field of view. Pitch, rate, volume, and intonation of the synthetic voice should be considered when choosing a particular speech synthesizer.

Contrast enhancement filters increase contrast and reduce glare from natural and overhead light sources. Screen enlargers provide magnification and attach to the computer monitor. Both are inexpensive devices and are available at local computer supply stores. Keyboard labels enlarge the size of letters from standard 18 point to 38 point size and numbers to 32 point.

Office equipment with speech recognition technology, braille labels, and other features has recently been developed to enable individuals who are visually impaired or blind to operate items such as photocopiers.

Braille uses the sense of touch as an alternative method of reading and writing. Raised dots in various combinations represent the letters of the alphabet, numbers, and punctuation. Braille text may be produced by using a braillewriter or a slate and stylus. Special computers use a braille device to produce either embossed paper output (braille) or paperless braille (a tactile display which uses retractable pins to form braille characters). Various software programs are used to convert text into files which produce braille output. Special portable devices enable people to take notes in braille while away from the office.

A significant addition to assistive technology for individuals who are visually impaired or blind is the optical character reader, which scans printed material and converts it to a machine-readable format that can be produced in braille or speech. Optical character readers are used in conjunction with character recognition software.

Many world wide web sites for individuals who are visually impaired or blind offer information in the latest technology, conferences, and job openings. With the use of a modem and a specially adapted computer, individuals who are visually impaired or blind may access these world wide web sites, receiving the data in large print, braille, or speech.

Computer access centers have been established at many public libraries and universities, where individuals may see the equipment and have "hands-on" experience before purchasing their own equipment. Some libraries will lend portable equipment to patrons. Information on obtaining financial assistance for the purchase of special equipment is discussed in Chapter 4, "Assistive Technology."

Another recent advance that utilizes computer technology is electronic publishing, which uses disks and CD-ROMs. To date, reference works such as dictionaries are the most commonly produced works on CD-ROM, although other types of books are coming on the market in this format as well. Since these publications are used with personal computers, they can be accessed by computers that have speech output systems.

Talking calculators, voice dialer telephones, audiocassette recorders, notetakers, audible labeling devices, and light probes (which help the individual find which phone line is ringing on a multi-line telephone) are examples of other assistive equipment used on the job by individuals who are visually impaired or blind.

Case Vignette

Sara Black, Using High Tech Aids to Remain Employed

Sara Black is a 30 year old woman who is legally blind due to diabetic retinopathy. The depression that accompanied her fluctuating vision caused Sara to consider resigning from her job as a receptionist/typist at a large publishing company. Kathy Turco, the director of disabilities management at the company, suggested that Sara make an appointment at the state agency that serves individuals who are visually impaired or blind. When Sara expressed trepidation about taking this step, Kathy introduced her to another employee who had recently been helped by the agency. After a lengthy discussion with her colleague, Sara decided to call her ophthalmologist and ask that he register her as legally blind, thereby setting the rehabilitation process in motion at the state agency.

Tom Wood, the social worker from the state agency, arranged a meeting with Sara at her home. About the same age as Sara, Tom is visually impaired from multiple sclerosis, a condition which also causes fluctuating vision. He described to Sara his own reactions to vision loss and how he adapted to the emotional aspects of vision impairment and coped with his work requirements.

Tom asked Sara to tell him about her major problems. She responded that she was uneasy about controlling her diabetes now that her vision was impaired and that she feared losing her job. Tom told Sara about a self-help group that was forming at the local chapter of the American Diabetes Association to help people with diabetes and vision loss cope with daily living, emotional responses, and the need to support themselves financially. Led by a nurse who had special training as a diabetes educator, the group required only that participants agree to attend all six initial sessions at the hospital and pay a minimal fee of ten dollars per session. After that time participants could decide whether to continue with additional group sessions. Tom also suggested a referral to a job accommodations specialist, which Sara gratefully accepted.

At her first group meeting, Sara found that several of the participants were about her age and encountering similar problems. With the help of Doris Tidwell, the nurse who was running the group, Sara learned about special syringes and blood glucose monitors with speech output that could help her monitor her

Continued on next page

diabetes. She also learned that her emotional reactions, which seemed to go to extremes, could have been caused by her inability to control her blood glucose properly. The group members discussed the difficulties in adjusting to vision that is poor one day, worse the next, and improved the following day. Sara was relieved to hear that her own reactions were not abnormal.

Terry Hart, the job accommodations consultant recommended by Tom Wood, arranged to meet with Sara at her place of employment to assess her specific situation. Although Sara was legally blind, she still had useful vision and would be able to continue typing by placing the material she needed to type under the camera of a closed circuit television which enlarged the material sufficiently for her to see it. Using this adaptive equipment in conjunction with a software program that enlarged the text on her computer monitor, Sara was able to continue typing. Terry also suggested improving the lighting on Sara's desk and rearranging the furniture in the office so that there were wide aisles with no protruding objects.

Terry helped Sara complete the application form from the state for financial assistance for purchasing the closed circuit television and the software program. Since the equipment was being used to enable Sara to retain her position, there would be no problem in securing this funding. Although Sara would be able to use this equipment as long as it was useful to her, title to the equipment would remain with the state.

Terry filed reports with both Tom Wood and Kathy Turco, the director of disability management at the company. She suggested that both conduct follow-up appointments with Sara every six months to determine if her situation was still satisfactory and whether any additional accommodations were necessary.

SUGGESTIONS FOR A SAFE AND FRIENDLY WORKPLACE

In addition to the sighted guide techniques described above, the following suggestions will help employers, co-workers, and employees who are visually impaired or blind feel more comfortable as they work together:

- Speak in a normal tone of voice. Unless the individual also has a hearing impairment, it is not necessary to speak loudly.

- When entering the office of an individual who is visually impaired or blind, always announce yourself by name. Entering an office quietly without saying anything can unpleasantly surprise a person who cannot see who is there. Always announce when you are leaving a room.

- Maintain eye contact with the person who is visually impaired or blind. Even though the individual may not be able to see your face, he or she will be able to tell the direction your voice is coming from and whether you are doing something else while talking.

- Shake the hand of a person who is visually impaired or blind in the same situations that you would shake the hand of a person with normal vision. Even if the person is unable to see an out-stretched hand, he or she will probably extend a hand in greeting. While shaking hands is common etiquette, it also serves to make contact with the individual who may not be able to make eye contact due to vision loss.

- Do not avoid using expressions such as "Do you *see* what I mean?" or words such as *look*. They are part of everyday language and are used comfortably by individuals who are visually impaired or blind.

- Avoid the tendency to use a third person as an intermediary when speaking to an individual who is visually impaired or blind. Speak directly to the individual; for example, do not ask, "Where does *he* or *she* want to go to lunch?" Rather, ask, "Where do *you* want to go to lunch?"

- In a meeting, ask each participant to introduce him or herself so that the individual who is visually impaired or blind will know who is present.

• Orient the individual to an unfamiliar setting with a description of the physical surroundings. Describe the arrangement of tables and chairs; where beverages are being served; and how to reach the restrooms, telephones, elevators, or escalators.

• When dining out, ask the individual if he or she would like you to read the menu. Read the prices! An individual who is blind may ask you to describe the location of the various foods on the plate.

• Do not play with a guide dog or contradict the owner's instructions to the dog. Never give food to a guide dog.

References

McNeil, John M.
2001   Americans With Disabilities 1997 Washington, DC: U.S. Bureau of the Census Current Population Reports P70-73

AFB National Technology Program
American Foundation for the Blind (AFB)
11 Penn Plaza, Suite 300
New York, NY 10001
(800) 232-5463   (212) 502-7642   FAX (212) 502-7773
techctr@afb.net   www.afb.org

This program conducts evaluations of assistive technology products, provides information on these projects, and coordinates the Careers and Technology Information Bank (see below).

American Council of the Blind (ACB)
1155 15th Street NW, Suite 1004
Washington, DC 20005
(800) 424-8666   (202) 467-5081   FAX (202) 467-5085
info@acb.org   www.acb.org

Membership organization with chapters in many states. Affiliated organizations representing special interests include the American Blind Lawyers Association, ACB Government Employees, and the National Alliance of Blind Teachers. Offers the ACB Jobs Bank, a listing of current jobs available, on the web site. The "Washington Connection," which provides news about legislation and employment, is available on the web site. Publishes the "Braille Forum," a monthly newsletter in large print, audiocassette, braille, via e-mail, and on the web site. Membership, $5.00.

Blinded Veterans Association (BVA)
477 H Street, NW
Washington, DC 20001-2694
(800) 669-7079   (202) 371-8880   bva@bva.org
www.bva.org

The BVA's field service and outreach employment programs help veterans find rehabilitation, services, training, and employment. Membership, $8.00, includes the "BVA Bulletin" in large print and on audiocassette. Also available on the web site.

Careers and Technology Information Bank (CTIB)
American Foundation for the Blind (AFB)
11 Penn Plaza, Suite 300
New York, NY 10001
(800) 232-5463   (212) 502-7642   FAX (212) 502-7773
techctr@afb.net   www.afb.org

This database lists individuals who are visually impaired or blind and their wide variety of professions and careers. The database serves as an information exchange on assistive technology, careers, education, and employment and is open to employers, individuals, parents, professionals, researchers, and engineers.

Department of Veterans Affairs Medical Centers (VA)
(800) 827-1000   www.va.gov

VA Medical Centers have established special Visual Impairment Service Teams (VIST) to provide rehabilitation services and assistive equipment to veterans with visual impairments. Contact the VA Medical Center in your geographical area. In some cases, veterans are referred to one of nine Blind Rehabilitation Centers or three Blind Rehabilitation Clinics for a short term residential rehabilitation program.

National Braille Association
3 Townline Circle
Rochester, NY 14623-2513
(585716) 428-8260   FAX (585716) 427-0263
nbaoffice@nationalbraille.rg
www.nationalbraille.org

Provides instruction and consultation to individuals and groups who transcribe print material to braille. Provides braille transcriptions of books, including career and technical materials. Maintains a depository of braille books that may be duplicated. Reader-Transcriber Registry matches braillists with individuals who need single copies of items for work, recreation, and daily living. Fees are based on the number of pages transcribed.

National Braille Press
88 St. Stephen Street
Boston, MA 02115
(888) 965-8965   (617) 266-6160   FAX (617) 437-0456
orders@nbp.org   www.nbp.org

Publishes computer guides and tutorials for word processing and database programs, spreadsheets, and CD-ROM in various formats, including print, audiocassette, PC disk, and braille. Free catalogue available in large print and braille. Also available on the web site.

Recording for the Blind and Dyslexic (RFB&D)
20 Roszel Road
Princeton, NJ 08540
(866) 732-3585   (800) 221-4792 (to order catalogue or books)
(609) 452-0606   FAX (609) 987-8116
custserv@rfbd.org   www.rfbd.org

Records educational materials, including employment related publications and computer manuals, for people who are legally blind or who have physical or perceptual disabilities. Available on audiocassette or CD. Requires certification of disability by a medical or educational professional. Registration fee, $65.00, Sells 4-track audiocassette players. Catalogue available online at www.rfbd.org/catalog.

Smith-Kettlewell Rehabilitation Engineering Research Center for Sensory Aids
2318 Fillmore Street
San Francisco, CA 94115
(415) 345-2000   FAX (415) 345-8455   www.ski.org

A federally funded center that develops and tests new technology for individuals who are visually impaired, blind, or deaf-blind. Provides some devices at cost; will provide schematics for others.

Trace Research and Development Center
University of Wisconsin-Madison
2107 Engineering Center Building
1550 Engineering Drive
Madison, WI 53706
(608) 262-6966   (608) 263-5408 (TTY)
FAX (608) 262-8848   info@trace.wisc.edu   trace.wisc.edu

Conducts research to make off the shelf technology more accessible to individuals with disabilities through universal design.

AccessWorld: Technology and People with Visual Impairments
American Foundation for the Blind (AFB)
11 Penn Plaza, Suite 300
New York, NY 10001
(800) 232-5463   (212) 502-7642   FAX (212) 502-7773
techctr@afb.net   www.afb.org/accessworld

A magazine that discusses products that can help individuals with visual impairments function in their daily lives. Available on the web site: www.afb.org/accessworld. Free

Assistive Devices for Use with Personal Computers
National Library Service for the Blind and Physically Handicapped (NLS)
1291 Taylor Street, NW
Washington, DC 20542
(800) 424-8567 or (800) 424-8572 (Reference Section)
(800) 424-9100 (to receive application)
(202) 707-5100   (202) 707-0744 (TTY)   FAX (202) 707-0712
nls@loc.gov   www.loc.gov/nls

This reference circular describes screen magnifiers, screen readers, web browsers, and other devices that convert print into synthetic speech. Includes list of vendors and bibliography. Free

Business Owners Who are Blind or Visually Impaired
by Deborah kendrick
AFB Press
PO Box 1020
Sewickley, PA 15143-1020
(800) 232-3044   FAX (412) 741-0609   abdorder@abdintl.com
www.afb.org

This book demonstrates the wide range of careers that individuals who are visually impaired or blind may enter. It profiles successful business owners in a variety of fields. $24.95

Careers & the DisABLED
Equal Opportunity Publications
445 Broad Hollow Road, Suite 425
Melville, NY 11747
(631) 421-9421   FAX (631) 421-0359   info@eop.com
www.eop.com

This quarterly magazine features career guidance articles, role model profiles, and lists of companies looking for qualified job candidates. Offers Online Resume Database which matches readers with advertisers who are recruiting employees. One year, $12.00; two years, $22.00.

Employed Ability: Blind Persons on the Job
AFB Press
PO Box 1020
Sewickley, PA 15143-1020
(800) 232-3044   FAX (412) 741-0609   abdorder@abdintl.com
www.afb.org

In this videotape, individuals who are visually impaired or blind discuss career opportunities and personal experiences in the workplace. Includes comments from employers and coworkers. 14 minutes. $49.95

Financial Aid for Students with Visual Impairments large print $30.00
Funding for Persons with Visual Impairments $50.00
Reference Service Press
5000 Windplay Drive, Suite 4
El Dorado Hills, CA 95762
(916) 939-9620   FAX (916) 939-9626   www.rspfunding.com

These books provide sources of scholarships and loans for students who are visually impaired and for individuals who are not in school.

Guide to Employment Resources for People with Impaired Vision
Lighthouse International
111 East 59th Street
New York, NY 10022
(800) 829-0500   (212) 821-9200   (212) 821-9713 (TTY)
FAX (212) 821-9705   www.lighthouse.org

This pamphlet lists employment resources, publications, and videos. Single copy, free. Also available on the web site.

Information on Grants-in-Aid for Persons Who Are Blind or Partially Sighted
Lighthouse International
111 East 59th Street
New York, NY 10022
(800) 829-0500   )   (212) 821-9200   (212) 821-9713 (TTY)
FAX (212) 821-9705   www.lighthouse.org

This brochure lists organizations that provide financial assistance for the purchase of assistive technology. Single copy, free. Also available on the web site.

Jobs to Be Proud Of: Profiles of Workers Who Are Blind or Visually Impaired
by Deborah Kendrick
AFB Press
PO Box 1020
Sewickley, PA 15143-1020
(800) 232-3044   FAX (412) 741-0609   abdorder@abdintl.com
www.afb.org

This book describes the jobs of 12 individuals and discusses their job choices and training. Offers practical strategies for employers and employees. Available in large print, audiocassette, and braille. $21.95

Living with Low Vision Series
Resources for Rehabilitation
22 Bonad Road
Winchester, Massachusetts 01890
(781) 368-9094   FAX (781) 368-9096   info@rfr.org
www.rfr.org

A series of publications designed to help professionals and consumers locate the products and services they need to function independently. Includes:

"Living with Low Vision: A Resource Guide for People with Sight Loss" is a large print comprehensive directory that helps people with sight loss remain independent. Describes services and products that enable individuals to keep reading, working, and carrying out daily activities. $46.95

"Meeting the Needs of People with Vision Loss: A Multidisciplinary Perspective"
Susan L. Greenblatt (ed.) Written by physicians, special educators, counselors, and rehabilitation professionals, this book includes chapters on What People with Vision Loss Need to Know; The Special Needs of Individuals with Diabetes and Vision Loss; Older Adults with Vision and Hearing Losses; Providing Services to Visually Impaired Elders in Long Term Care Facilities; Children with Vision Loss; and The Role of the Family. $24.95

"Providing Services for People with Vision Loss: A Multidisciplinary Perspective"
Susan L. Greenblatt (ed.) A collection of articles by ophthalmologists, rehabilitation professionals, a sociologist and a physician who is visually impaired. Chapters include Vision Loss: A Patient's Perspective; Vision Loss: An Ophthalmologist's Perspective; Operating a Low Vision Aids Service; The Need for Coordinated Care; Making Referrals for Rehabilita-tion Services; Mental Health Services: The Missing Link; Self-Help Groups for People with Sight Loss. $19.95

<u>Magazines on Audiocassette</u>
Associated Services for the Blind
919 Walnut Street, 2nd Floor
Philadelphia, PA 19107
(215) 627-0600, extension 208   FAX (215) 922-0692
www.asb.org

Subscriptions on 4-track audiocassette for popular computer magazines such as "Computers," "Computerworld," and "Macuser" which are not available in special media elsewhere. Free price list.

<u>Microsoft Word for Windows</u>
National Braille Press
88 St. Stephen Street
Boston, MA 02115
(800) 548-7323   (617) 266-6160   FAX (617) 437-0456
orders@nbp.org   www.nbp.org

This software program offers beginning Word users a step-by-step tutorial. ASCII text on floppy disk. $10.00

<u>A Practical Guide to the ADA and Visual Impairment</u>
by Elga Joffee
AFB Press
PO Box 1020
Sewickley, PA 15143-1020
(800) 232-3044   FAX (412) 741-0609   abdorder@abdintl.com
www.afb.org

This book provides information to help businesses, architects, and facilities planners implement the ADA for individuals who are blind or visually impaired. It includes information on accommodations that may be required when hiring a blind or visually impaired employee, a list of government agencies to contact regarding specific sections of the ADA, and resources for purchasing products. $39.95

<u>Preparing for College and Beyond</u>
Virginia M. Woolf Foundation
1658 Fifth Street
Manhattan Beach, CA 90266
(310) 379-8321   FAX (310) 372-2943   info@text-key.com
www.text-key.com

This book helps high school students who are blind or visually impaired learn how to complete applications for college, register, understand schedules and catalogues, obtain textbooks in braille, write research projects, and take tests. On CD. $29.95

Resources for People with Disabilities and Chronic Conditions
Resources for Rehabilitation
22 Bonad Road
Winchester, Massachusetts 01890
(781) 368-9094   FAX (781) 368-9096   info@rfr.org
www.rfr.org

A comprehensive resource guide with chapters on vision impairment, spinal cord injuries, low back pain, diabetes, multiple sclerosis, Parkinson's disease, hearing and speech impairments, and epilepsy. Includes information about the disease or condition; psychological aspects of the condition; professional service providers; environmental adaptations; assistive devices; and descriptions of organizations, publications, and products. $56.95 (See order form on last page of this book.)

Skills for Success: A Career Education Handbook for Children and Adolescents with Visual Impairments
by Karen E. Wolffe
AFB Press
PO Box 1020
Sewickley, PA 15143-1020
(800) 232-3044   (412) 741-1398
FAX (412) 741-0609   afbpress@afb.org   www.afb.org

This guide offers suggestions that will enable children with visual impairments to develop life skills that will lead to successful careers. $45.95

Students Who Are Blind or Visually Impaired in Postsecondary Education
HEATH Resource Center
George Washington University
2121 K Street, NW, Suite 220
Washington, DC 20037
(800) 544-3284 (V/TTY)   (202) 973-0904 (V/TTY)
FAX (202) 973-0908   askheath@heath.gwu.edu   www.heath.gwu.edu

Designed for students, family members, and service providers, this brief paper describes the rights of students at postsecondary institutions and the services that they provide. Free. Also available on the web site.

Voice Recognition Technology
PACER Center (Parent Advocacy Coalition for Educational Rights)
8161 Normandale Boulevard
Minneapolis, MN 55437
(888) 248-0822   (952) 838-9000
In MN, (800) 537-2237   (952) 838-0190 (TTY)
FAX (952) 838-0199   pacer@pacer.org   www.pacer.org

This publication discusses how voice recognition can help people with disabilities. It discusses the latest technology and provides a list of vendors and web sites. $3.00

Windows XP Explained
National Braille Press
88 St. Stephen Street
Boston, MA 02115
(800) 548-7323   (617) 266-6160   FAX (617) 437-0456
orders@nbp.org   www.nbp.org

This software program offers both basic and advanced concepts of Windows as well as a list of keyboard commands. ASCII text on floppy disk. $20.00

Work Sight
Braille Institute of America, Inc.
741 North Vermont Avenue
Los Angeles, CA 90029-9988
(800) 272-4553
webmaster@reachout.org   www.brailleinstitute.org

In this videotape, individuals who are visually impaired describe their transition to the workplace. Emotional and psychological adjustments as well as a team approach to problem-solving are discussed. Free

VENDORS OF ASSISTIVE DEVICES

Listed below are manufacturers of assistive devices and mail order catalogues that specialize in devices for people who are visually impaired or blind. Unless otherwise noted, catalogues are in standard print, include a variety of products, and are free.

Ai Squared
PO Box 669
Manchester Center, VT 05255-0669
(800) 85902702   FAX (802) 362-1670   support@aisquared.com
www.aisquared.com

Produces screen magnification software. Big Shot is for Windows and ZoomText for DOS.

American Printing House for the Blind (APH)
PO Box 6085
Louisville, KY 40206-0085
(800) 223-1839   (502) 895-2405   FAX (502) 899-2274
info@aph.org   www.aph.org

Sells the Orion TI-34 Talking Scientific Calculator that performs scientific functions with speech output. Also sells the Book Port, a hand-held device that can download electronic text and provide speech output.

American Thermoform
1758 Brackett Street
LaVerne, CA 91750
(800) 331-3676   (909) 593-6711   FAX (909) 593-8001
rhaggen@americanthermoform.com   www.atcbrleqp.com

Manufactures equipment which enables PC users to read the screen display in braille format; braille printers compatible with both PCs and Macintosh computers; printers that print both braille and standard print simultaneously; and special papers necessary for printing braille.

Artic Technologies
1000 John R Road, Suite 108
Troy, MI 48083
(248) 588-7370   FAX (248) 588-2650
info@artictech.com   www.artictech.com

Produces TransType notetaker with speech synthesis and screen access systems including hardware, software, voice tutorials, and accessories.

Blazie Engineering
109 East Jarrettsville Road, Unit D
Forest Hill, MD 21050
(410) 893-9333   FAX (410) 836-5040   www.blazie.com

Sells portable talking braille notetakers, braille monitors, braille printers, braille translators, specialized software, Windows screen readers, and speech synthesizers. The TransType is a notetaker keyboard with speech output.

Duxbury Systems
270 Littleton Road, Unit 6
Westford, MA 01886
(800) 347-9594   (978) 692-3000
FAX (978) 692-7912   info@duxsys.com
www.duxburysystems.com

The Duxbury Brailler is software that translates print to braille and vice versa for Windows, DOS, and Macintosh. MegaDots is a braille translation and word processing software for literary, mathematical, and scientific applications. Compatible with speech and screen enlargement programs.

Enabling Technology
1601 NE Braille Place
Jensen Beach, L 34957
(800 777-3687   FAX (800)950-3687   (772) 225-3687
FAX (772) 225-3299   enabling@brailler.com   www.brailler.com

Designs, manufactures, and supports braille embossers.

Enhanced Vision
17911 Sampson Lane
Huntington Beach, CA 92647
(800) 440-9476   (714) 465-3400   (714) 374-1821
info@enhancedvision.com   www.enhancedvision.com

Produces Merlin, a video magnifier in various sizes and options; Jordy, a portable system that magnifies images onto a set of glasses; Flipper, a magnification system that hooks up to televisions and monitors and projects the image onto glasses; and Max, a portable digital magnifier that connects to televisions and computers.

Florida New Concepts Marketing
PO Box 261
Port Richey, FL 34673-0261
(727) 842-3231 (V/FAX)   staff@skyport.com   gulfside.com/compulenz

Produces Compu-Lenz, which enlarges character size while eliminating distortion and light reflection. Fits on most computer monitors.

Franklin Electronic Publishers, Inc.
1 Franklin Road
Burlington, NJ 08016-4907
(800) 266-5626   FAX (609) 239-5948   service@franklin.com
www.franklin.com

Publishes "stand alone" systems with speech output that have dictionaries, thesauruses, and other nonfiction and fiction works.

Freedom Scientific
11800 31st Court North
St. Petersburg, FL 33716-1805
(800) 336-5658   (727) 803-8000   FAX (727) 803-8001
info@freedomscientific.com   www.freedomscientfic.com

Produces a variety of high tech devices that enable the use of Windows and screen readers with braille or speech output. JAWS (Job Access With Speech) is a screen access software program designed to interact with Microsoft Windows. MAGic is a magnification software for PCs. Cassette tutorials and training programs available. PAC Mate is a hand-held personal data assistant that allows the user to have access to the Internet or read books with braille display or speech output. Available with standard or braille keyboard.

GW Micro
725 Airport North Office Park
Fort Wayne, IN 46825
(260) 489-3671   FAX (260) 489-2608
support@gwmicro.com   www.gwmicro.com

Sells speech synthesizers, screen readers, and speech recognition software for PCs. Large print, audiocassette, and disk instruction manuals available. Also sells other vendors' computer systems, synthesizers, software, and accessories. Newsletter, "Voice of Vision," available on the web site. Free

Hooleon Corporation
PO Box 589
Melrose, NM 88124
(800) 937-1337   (505) 253-4503   FAX (505) 853-4299
webmaster@hooleon.com   www.hooleon.com

Produces keyboard labels that enlarge the size of letters from standard 18 point to 38 point size and numbers to 32 point. Black print on ivory or yellow and white print on black. Braille keytop labels with or without labels and home-row indicators are also available.

IBM Accessibility Center
11400 Burnet Road
Austin, TX 78758
(800) 426-4832   www.ibm.com/able

Produces a variety of software programs that enable people who are visually impaired or blind to access personal computers. Home Page Reader is a talking web browser is available for use with Microsoft Windows. The Screen Reader/DOS is compatible with DOS and produces speech output of screen text.

Independent Living Aids, Inc. (ILA)
200 Robbins Lane
Jericho, NY 11753
(800) 537-2118   (516) 937-1848   FAX (516) 937-3906
can-do@independentliving.com   www.independentliving.com

Sells a variety of low tech and high tech devices.

LS & S Group
PO Box 673
Northbrook, IL 60065
(800) 468-4789   (866) 317-8533 (TTY)
(847) 498-9777   FAX (847) 498-1482
info@LSSproducts.com   www.lssgroup.com

Sells a variety of low tech and high tech devices.

Optelec
321 Billerica Road
Chelmsford, MA 01824
(800) 828-1056   FAX (800) 929-2444
customerservice@optelec.com   www.optelec.com

Produces the Clear View series of monitors that magnify up to 44 times and come with a variety of options. The Braille Voyager produces a braille display and works with both Windows and DOS. Also sells hand-held, stand, and illuminated magnifiers, lamps, and products for everyday living.

Pulse Data HumanWare, Inc.
175 Mason Circle
Concord, CA 94520
(800) 722-3393   (925) 680-7100   FAX (925) 681-4630
usa@pulsedata.com   www.pulsedata.com

Produces and sells speech synthesizers; scan and read systems; software for individuals with visual impairment and learning disabilities; braille displays; notetakers; embossers, and translation devices; and screen access software.

ScanSoft Company
9 Centennial Drive
Peabody, MA 01960
(978) 977-2000   www.scansoft.com

Produces the Dragon NaturallySpeaking software system, which converts dictated speech into text in a Windows application.

Science Products
PO Box 888
Southeastern, PA 19399
(800) 888-7400   FAX (610) 296-0488   cappekinc@concast.net

"Vision Aids Resource Guide" offers optical and nonoptical aids, including scientific, statistical, or financial calculators and telephone aids, such as a talking caller ID and telephone light sensor. Operates CAPTEK, which custom designs assistive equipment, such as talking cash registers, tools, and bar code readers.

TeleSensory
520 Almanor Avenue
Sunnyvale, CA 94086-3533
(800) 804-8004   (408) 616-8700   FAX (408) 616-8720
info@telesensory.com   www.telesensory.com

Produces personal reading and computer magnification systems and optical character recognition equipment. Produces the Aladdin series of video magnifiers with varying sizes of monitors and features. Ovation scans printed matter and converts it into speech output.

TRAINING PROGRAMS

Carroll Center for the Blind Computer Training Services Program
770 Centre Street
Newton, MA 02458
(800) 852-3131   (617) 969-6200   FAX (617) 969-6204
webmaster@carroll.org   www.carroll.org

Offers evaluation and training in use of large print, speech, and braille output equipment. Housing available. Online courses available at www.carrolltech.org.

Computer Center for Visually Impaired People
Baruch College
1 Bernard Baruch Way, Box 648
New York, NY 10010
(646) 312-1420   FAX (212) 802-2103
www.baruch.cuny.edu/ccvip

Training courses in the use of personal computers and popular software programs; career counseling; internships; and courses for professionals.

Hadley School for the Blind
700 Elm Street
Winnetka, IL 60093
(800) 323-4238   In IL, (847) 446-8111
FAX (847) 446-8153   www.hadley-school.org

Correspondence courses on computers and word processing for individuals who are legally blind. Free

Lions World Services for the Blind
2811 Fair Park Boulevard
Little Rock, AR 72214
(800) 248-0734   (501) 664-7100   FAX (501) 664-2743
training@lwsb.org   www.lwsb.org

Courses in computer programming, word processing, and other software packages. Housing available.

STORER Computer Access Center
Sight Center, Cleveland Society for the Blind
1909 East 101st Street
Cleveland, OH 44106
(216) 791-8118   FAX (216) 791-1101
www.clevelandsightcenter.org

Evaluation and training center for use of equipment with large print, voice, and braille output. Housing available.

University of New Orleans Training, Resource and Assistive Technology Center
PO Box 1051
New Orleans, LA 70148
(504) 280-5700 (V/TTY)   FAX (504) 280-5707   www.uno.edu/~trac

Academic year and summer continuing education courses in word processing, database management, medical transcription, and Lotus. Vocational evaluations, assistive technology assessment, job readiness training, and job placement available.

INDEX OF ORGANIZATIONS

This index contains only those organizations listed under sections titled "ORGANIZATIONS." These organizations may also be listed as vendors of publications, tapes, and other products.

Publications from Resources for Rehabilitation

Meeting the Needs of Employees with Disabilities

This resource guide provides the information people with disabilities need to retain or obtain employment. Includes information on government programs and laws such as the Americans with Disabilities Act, training programs, supported employment, transition from school to work, assistive technology, and environmental adaptations. Chapters on hearing and speech impairments, mobility impairments, and visual impairment and blindness describe organizations, adaptive equipment, and services plus suggestions for a safe and friendly workplace. Case vignettes describing accommodations for employees with disabilities are a new special feature.

Fourth edition, 2004   ISBN 0-929718-34-8 $46.95

"...solid and up-to-date."   *Journal of Career Planning and Employment*
"...an excellent directory for those challenged with incorporating persons with disabilities in the workplace..."
AAOHN Journal
"...recommended for public libraries and for academic libraries..."
Choice
"...a timely resource." American Reference Books Annual

A Woman's Guide to Coping with Disability

This <u>unique</u> book addresses the special needs of women with disabilities and chronic conditions, such as social relationships, sexual functioning, pregnancy, childrearing, caregiving, and employment. Special attention is paid to ways in which women can advocate for their rights with the health care and rehabilitation systems. Written for women in all age categories, the book has chapters on the disabilities that are most prevalent in women or likely to affect the roles and physical functions unique to women. Included are arthritis, coronary heart disease, diabetes, epilepsy, lupus, multiple sclerosis, osteoporosis, and spinal cord injury. Each chapter also includes information about the condition, professional service providers, and psychological aspects plus descriptions of organizations, publications and tapes, and special assistive devices. This new edition includes e-mail addresses and Internet resources. Fourth edition, 2003   ISBN 0-929718-33-x $46.95

"...this excellent, empowering resource belongs in all collections." Library Journal
"...crucial information women need to be informed, empowered, and in control of their lives. Excellent self-help information... Highly recommended for public and academic libraries." Choice
"...a marvelous publication...will help women feel more in control of their lives." A nurse who became disabled

A Man's Guide to Coping with Disability

Written to fill the void in the literature regarding the special needs of men with disabilities, this book includes information about men's responses to disability, with a special emphasis on the values men place on independence, occupational achievement, and physical activity. Information on finding local services, self-help groups, laws that affect men with disabilities, sports and recreation, and employment is applicable to men with any type of disability or chronic condition. The disabilities that are most prevalent in men or that affect men's special roles in society are included. Chapters on coronary heart disease, diabetes, HIV/AIDS, multiple sclerosis, prostate conditions, spinal cord injury, and stroke include information about the disease or condition, psychological aspects, sexual functioning, where to find services, environmental adaptations, and annotated entries of organizations, publications and tapes, and resources for assistive devices. Includes e-mail addresses and Internet resources.

Third edition, 2003   ISBN 0-929718-32-1 $46.95

"a unique reference source." Library Journal
"a unique purchase for public libraries" Booklist/Reference Books Bulletin

The Mental Health Resource Guide

In a landmark report, the Surgeon General declared that mental illness is a public health problem of great magnitude. Both the public and professionals hold misconceptions about mental disorders. **The Mental Health Resource Guide** is designed to help individuals who are mentally ill, family members, and health professionals understand the issues surrounding mental illness and find services. The book provides information on treatments in current use, medications, laws that affect individuals who are mentally ill, employment, and the needs of children and elders. The effects of mental illness on the family and caregivers are also addressed. Chapters on anxiety disorders, eating disorders, depressive disorders, schizophrenia, and substance abuse include information about causes, diagnoses, and treatments as well as descriptions of helpful organizations, publications, and tapes. Includes Internet resources.

2001   ISBN 0-929718-27-5 $39.95

"...authoritative...will add value to professional health care collections and public libraries."
                                                    Library Journal
"packed full of information...in crisp, clear prose."   **American Reference Books Annual**

Resources for Elders with Disabilities

This book meets the needs of elders, family members, and other caregivers. Published in LARGE PRINT, the book provides information about rehabilitation, laws that affect elders with disabilities, and self-help groups. Each chapter that deals with a specific disability or condition has information on the causes and treatments for the condition; psychological aspects; professional service providers; where to find services; environmental adaptations; and suggestions for making everyday living safer and easier. Chapters on hearing loss, vision loss, Parkinson's disease, stroke, arthritis, osteoporosis, and diabetes also provide information on organizations, publications and tapes, and assistive devices. Throughout the book are practical suggestions to prevent accidents and to facilitate interactions with family members, friends, and service providers. Plus information about aids for everyday living, older workers, falls, travel, and housing.

Fifth edition, 2002   ISBN 0-929718-31-3 $51.95

"...especially useful for older readers. Highly recommended." Library Journal
"...a valuable, well organized, easy-to-read reference source." American Reference Books Annual
"...a handy ready-reference..."   **Reference Books Bulletin/Booklist**

Making Wise Medical Decisions
How to Get the Information You Need

This book includes a **wealth** of information about where to go and what to read in order to make wise medical decisions. The book describes a plan for obtaining relevant health information and evaluating health facilities. Each chapter includes extensive resources to help the reader get started. Chapters include Getting the Information You Need to Make Wise Medical Decisions; Locating Appropriate Health Care; Asking the Right Questions about Medical Tests and Procedures; Protecting Yourself in the Hospital; Medical Benefits and Legal Rights; Drugs; Protecting the Health of Children Who Are Ill; Special Issues Facing Elders; People with Chronic Illnesses and Disabilities and the Health Care System; Making Decisions about Current Medical Controversies; Terminal Illness. Includes e-mail addresses and Internet resources.

Second edition, 2001   ISBN 0-929718-29-1 $42.95

"It is refreshing to find a source of practical information on how to proceed through the medical maze...this should become a popular resource in any public, hospital, or academic library's consumer health collection." Library Journal
"The book is very, very good. There's so much information, it's definitely worth buying." A health care consumer

Living with Low Vision: A Resource Guide for People with Sight Loss

This LARGE PRINT (18 point bold type) comprehensive guide helps people with sight loss locate the services, products, and publications that they need to keep reading, working, and enjoying life. Chapters for children and elders plus information on self-help groups, how to keep reading and working with vision loss, and making everyday living easier. Information on laws that affect people with vision loss, including the ADA, and high tech equipment that promotes independence and employment. Includes e-mail addresses and Internet resources.

Sixth edition, 2001   ISBN 0-929718-28-3 $46.95

"No other complete resource guide exists..an invaluable tool for locating services.. for public and academic libraries."
Library Journal
"...a good reference for libraries serving visually handicapped individuals."
American Reference Books Annual
"...a very useful resource for patients experiencing vision loss."   Archives of Ophthalmology
"...a superb resource...should be made available in waiting rooms or patient education areas..."
American Journal of Ophthalmology
"This volume is a treasure chest of concise, useful information."   OT Week

Resources for People with Disabilities and Chronic Conditions

This comprehensive resource guide has chapters on spinal cord injury, low back pain, diabetes, multiple sclerosis, hearing and speech impairments, vision impairment and blindness, and epilepsy. Each chapter includes information about the disease or condition; psychological aspects of the condition; professional service providers; environmental adaptations; assistive devices; and descriptions of organizations, publications, and products. Chapters on rehabilitation services, independent living, self-help, laws that affect people with disabilities (including the ADA), and making everyday living easier. Special information for children is also included. Includes e-mail addresses and Internet resources. Fifth edition 2002   ISBN 0-929718-30-5 $56.95

"...wide coverage and excellent organization of this encyclopedic guide...recommended..." Choice
"Sensitive to the tremendous variety of needs and circumstances of living with a disability."   American Libraries
"...an excellent resource for consumers and professionals..." Journal of the American Paraplegia Society
"...improves the chances of library patrons finding needed services..." American Reference Books Annual

Providing Services for People with Vision Loss: A Multidisciplinary Perspective

This book discusses how various professionals can work together to provide coordinated care. Chapters include Vision Loss: A Patient's Perspective; Vision Loss: An Ophthalmologist's Perspective; Operating a Low Vision Aids Service; The Need for Coordinated Care; Making Referrals for Rehabilitation Services; Mental Health Services: The Missing Link; Self-Help Groups for People with Sight Loss. Also available on cassette.

1989   ISBN 0-929718-02-X $19.95

"...an excellent guide for professionals."   **Journal of Rehabilitation**

Meeting the Needs of People with Vision Loss: A Multidisciplinary Perspective

This book discusses how to provide appropriate information and how to serve special populations. Chapters include What People with Vision Loss Need to Know; Information and Referral Services; The Role of the Family in the Adjustment to Blindness or Visual Impairment; Diabetes and Vision Loss; Special Needs of Children and Adolescents; Older Adults with Vision and Hearing Losses; Providing Services to Visually Impaired Elders in Long Term Care Facilities.

1991   ISBN 0-929718-07-0 $24.95

"...of use to anyone concerned with improving service delivery to the growing population of people who are visually impaired."   American Journal of Occupational Therapy

RESOURCES for REHABILITATION →

22 Bonad Road ● Winchester, MA 01890
(781) 368-9094 ● FAX (781) 368-9096 ● orders@rfr.org ● www.rfr.org
Our Federal Employer Identification Number is 04-2975-007

NAME _____

ORGANIZATION _____

ADDRESS _____

PHONE _____ E-MAIL ADDRESS: _____

[ ] Check or signed institutional purchase order enclosed for full amount of order. Purchase orders accepted from government agencies, hospitals, and universities <u>only</u>.

[ ] Mastercard/VISA Card number: _____

Signature: _____ Expiration date: _____

ALL ORDERS OF $100.00 OR LESS <u>MUST</u> BE PREPAID.

TITLE	QUANTITY		PRICE	TOTAL
A Woman's Guide to Coping with Disability	____	X	$46.95	_____
A Man's Guide to Coping with Disability	____	X	46.95	_____
The Mental Health Resource Guide	____	X	39.95	_____
Meeting the Needs of Employees with Disabilities	____	X	46.95	_____
Resources for People with Disabilities and Chronic Conditions	____	X	56.95	_____
Resources for Elders with Disabilities	____	X	51.95	_____
Making Wise Medical Decisions	____	X	42.95	_____
Living with Low Vision: A Resource Guide	____	X	46.95	_____
Providing Services for People with Vision Loss	____	X	19.95	_____
Meeting the Needs of People with Vision Loss	____	X	24.95	_____

SUB-TOTAL _____

SHIPPING & HANDLING: $50.00 or less, add $5.00; $50.01 to 100.00, add $8.00;
add $4.00 for each additional $100.00 or fraction of $100.00. Alaska, Hawaii,
U.S. territories, and Canada, add $3.00 to shipping and handling charges.
Foreign orders must be prepaid in U.S. currency. Please write for shipping charges.

SHIPPING/HANDLING _____

<u>Prices are subject to change.</u>

TOTAL $_____

During the <u>15 years</u> that Resources for Rehabilitation has been publishing books, we have received consistently high praise from reviewers and consumers alike:

"The place to go when you need to know." American Libraries

"Highly recommended." Library Journal

"Sensitive to the tremendous variety of needs and circumstances of living with a disability." American Libraries

"...crucial information women need to be informed, empowered, and in control of their lives. Excellent self-help information... Highly recommended" Choice

*"I got this book from my public library and **wanted to buy a copy for myself.**"* A health care consumer

"Wide coverage and excellent organization of this encyclopedic guide... recommended. Choice